COMMUNITY PRIMARY SCHOOL

10 minute

Maths
Assessments

for ages 10-11

CONTENTS

Assessment for learning

It is widely acknowledged that effective learning takes place where teachers understand their pupils' standards of achievement and lead the pupils forwards from these standards.

> *Assessment for learning is the process of seeking and interpreting evidence for use by learners and their teachers to decide where the learners are in their learning, where they need to go and how best to get there.*
>
> (Assessment for Learning: 10 principles – Assessment Reform Group)

This book will help you to assess your pupils' progress by providing activities that are quick and easy to administer, that can be used on a regular basis and that will help you build a profile of each pupil's attainment. Each activity will provide you with evidence of achievement that you can use for on-going pupil assessment and will help you focus your teaching and planning on the specific learning requirements of each child in your class.

Using the materials in this book will provide opportunities for both formative and summative assessment. It is recommended that the activities are used on a regular basis as part of an ordinary maths lesson, for continuous formative assessment. Recording the progress of each pupil, using the recording grid provided, will also assist you in making regular summative assessments in relation to National Curriculum levels of attainment.

All aspects of the *Framework for mathematics* for Year 6 are addressed through the assessment of separate learning objectives. These learning objectives are drawn from Strands 2 to 7 of the Framework:

2. Counting and understanding number
3. Knowing and using number facts
4. Calculating
5. Understanding shape
6. Measuring
7. Handling data

Many of the activities can also be used to support your assessment of Strand 1 (*Using and applying mathematics*). The teachers' notes accompanying each activity indicate where an assessment is particularly relevant to this.

How to use the activities for assessing pupils' progress

Ideally, pupils will work with an adult on an individual basis or in a very small group to enable the adult to make effective judgements about each individual's achievement. Everything achieved by the pupil should be a learning experience, perhaps where a particular skill or an aspect of knowledge is being strengthened and consolidated, or where a style of layout or method is being encountered for the first time. However, the assessment activities should only be used when the pupil has some prior experience of the work being assessed.

A pupil may be able to complete some, but not all, of the learning objectives. Any adult working closely with a pupil may discover 'gaps' in their understanding that can be reported back to the class teacher for monitoring and planning purposes. Further practice, focusing on specific areas, will help to fill these gaps and the assessment can then be repeated when the pupil is ready.

What's on the CD

The CD that accompanies this book can be used on a computer or CD player and features an audio track that can be used for the assessments that require audio. Children are often more focused when listening to a recording as the sound of a different voice helps to hold their attention. The teachers' notes for each assessment indicate whether there is an accompanying audio track and its number on the CD.

The CD also includes a recording grid on which you can indicate whether individual children have achieved specific learning objectives. You may decide not to use all the assessments with every pupil. In some cases, you might feel that you already have sufficient evidence that a child has achieved the specific objective and so leave it out. You may also decide to complete the assessments in a different order from the order in this book.

By filling in the the recording grid you will be able to build a clear picture of an individual's strengths and weaknesses as well as the class as a whole. The recording grid can be used to form an evidence base for assessing the National Curriculum level of each pupil, i.e. summative assessment. Your school or local authority will provide guidance regarding interpretation of evidence to make decisions about pupils' levels. Each pupil will be deemed to have reached a 'low', 'secure' or 'high' standard against the level criteria. Our recording grid uses these 'standards' (with red for 'low', orange for 'secure' and green for 'high') in relation to each 'I can' statement to help you make appropriate decisions about the progress of each pupil and how you might focus your teaching on each pupil's learning requirements.

Note that assessments are **not** provided for the following statements from the *Framework for mathematics* as these can be adequately covered in day-to-day experiences:

- Describe, identify and visualise parallel and perpendicular edges or faces; use these properties to classify 2-D shapes and 3-D solids

- Make and draw shapes with increasing accuracy and apply knowledge of their properties

- Read and interpret scales on a range of measuring instruments

- Solve problems by collecting, selecting, processing, presenting and interpreting data, using ICT where appropriate

Find the difference between positive and negative integers

Building on previous learning

Before starting this unit check that the children can already:
- count from any given number in whole number and decimal steps, extending beyond zero when counting backwards.
- relate any given number to its position on a number line.

Learning objectives

Objective 1: Find the difference between a positive and a negative integer in context.

Learning outcomes

The children will be able to:
- demonstrate their ability to find the difference between negative and positive integers in relation to temperature.
- demonstrate their ability to find the difference between negative and positive integers through reference to a number line.

Success criteria

The children have a **secure** level of attainment in relation to Objective 1 if the following questions can be answered with a 'yes'.

Can the children…

… find differences in temperature, using the appropriate vocabulary confidently e.g. 'minus four degrees Celsius'.

… use the number line to find differences between positive and negative integers, using confidently the appropriate vocabulary for negative numbers i.e. 'minus four' or 'negative four', and realise that some people use either or both of these terms interchangeably?

Administering the assessment

🔘 Track 1 Ensure that the children understand the task and help them read the questions if necessary. The assessment relies on the CD for a timed test where the children are given ten seconds to answer each question. The children can use the 'working out space' on the test sheet if they need to. This is the script for the CD if you decide to dictate the questions (the answers are provided after each question below).

I will say each question twice then you will have ten seconds to answer it.
Question 1: Find the difference in temperature between London and New York.   7°C
Question 2: What is the difference in temperature between Muscat and Edinburgh?   39°C
Question 3: What is the difference in temperature between Sydney and Moscow?   34°C
Question 4: What is the difference in temperature between Stockholm and Nice?   17°C
Question 5: Find the difference in temperature between Muscat and New York.   38°C
Question 6: Find the difference in temperature between London and Stockholm.   11°C
Question 7: How much more is 5 than negative 3?   8
Question 8: How much less than 1 is minus 1?   2
Question 9: What is the difference between 6 and negative 7?   13
Question 10: How much more than minus 8 is minus 2?   6
Question 11: How much less than 10 is negative 10?   20
Question 12: Calculate the difference between negative 6 and 9.   15

(This assessment will also provide evidence for assessing strand 1, Using and applying mathematics: Represent and interpret sequences, patterns and relationships involving numbers; Explain reasoning and conclusions, using words, symbols or diagrams as appropriate.)

Andrew Brodie: Ten Minute Maths Assessments ages 10–11 © A&C Black 2009

Find the difference between positive and negative integers

Name

Date

Look at the temperatures in eight different cities.
Listen carefully to the CD or your teacher.

London 4°C   New York −3°C   Muscat 35°C
Edinburgh −4°C   Sydney 22°C   Moscow −12°C
Stockholm −7°C   Nice 10°C

1. ( )   **3.** ( )   **5.** ( )

2. ( )   **4.** ( )   **6.** ( )

−10 −9 −8 −7 −6 −5 −4 −3 −2 −1 0 1 2 3 4 5 6 7 8 9 10

7. ( )   5   −3   Working out space

8. ( )   1   −1

9. ( )   6   −7

10. ( )   −8   −2

11. ( )   10   −10

12. ( )   −6   9

I can find differences between positive and negative numbers in relation to temperature.

I can find differences between positive and negative numbers by using a number line.

Andrew Brodie: Ten Minute Maths Assessments ages 10–11 © A&C Black 2009

Use decimal notation for tenths, hundredths and thousandths

Building on previous learning

Before starting this unit check that the children can already:

- explain what each digit represents in whole numbers and decimals with up to two places, and partition, round and order these numbers.

Learning objectives

Objective 1: Use decimal notation for tenths, hundredths and thousandths.

Learning outcomes

The children will be able to:

- write fractions given in tenths, hundredths or thousandths as decimal numbers.

Success criteria

The children have a **secure** level of attainment in relation to Objective 1 if the following questions can be answered with a yes:

Can the children write...

... tenths as decimals?

... hundredths as decimals, recognising that 43 hundredths is shown as 4 tenths and 3 hundredths in decimal form?

... thousandths as decimals, recognising that 63 thousandths is shown as 6 hundredths and 3 thousandths and that 729 is shown as 7 tenths, 2 hundredths and 9 thousandths in decimal form?

Administering the assessment

Track 2 Ensure that the children understand the task and help them read the questions if necessary. The assessment relies on the CD for a timed test where the children are given ten seconds to answer each question. This is the script for the CD if you decide to dictate the questions (the answers are provided after each question below).

I will say each question twice then you will have ten seconds to answer it.

Question 1: Write the fraction 6 tenths as a decimal.	*0.6*
Question 2: Write the fraction 9 tenths as a decimal.	*0.9*
Question 3: Write the fraction 7 hundredths as a decimal.	*0.07*
Question 4: Write the fraction 2 hundredths as a decimal.	*0.02*
Question 5: Write the fraction 5 thousandths as a decimal.	*0.005*
Question 6: Write the fraction 8 thousandths as a decimal.	*0.008*
Question 7: Write the fraction 19 hundredths as a decimal.	*0.19*
Question 8: Write the fraction 43 hundredths as a decimal.	*0.43*
Question 9: Write the fraction 99 hundredths as a decimal.	*0.99*
Question 10: Write the fraction 11 thousandths as a decimal.	*0.011*
Question 11: Write the fraction 63 thousandths as a decimal.	*0.063*
Question 12: Write the fraction 729 thousandths as a decimal.	*0.729*

(This assessment will also provide evidence for assessing strand 1, Using and applying mathematics: Represent and interpret sequences, patterns and relationships involving numbers; Explain reasoning and conclusions, using words, symbols or diagrams as appropriate.)

Andrew Brodie: Ten Minute Maths Assessments ages 10–11 © A&C Black 2009

Use decimal notation for tenths, hundredths and thousandths

Name

Date

One tenth can be written like this: $\frac{1}{10}$ or like this: **0.1**

One hundredth can be written like this: $\frac{1}{100}$ or like this: **0.01**

One thousandth can be written like this: $\frac{1}{1000}$ or like this: **0.001**

Listen to the CD or your teacher. Write the fractions as decimals.

1.

2.

3.

4.

5.

6.

7.

8.

9.

10.

11.

12.

I can use decimal notation for tenths, hundredths and thousandths.

Partition decimals with up to three places

Building on previous learning

Before starting this unit check that the children can already:
- explain what each digit represents in whole numbers and decimals with up to two places, and partition, round and order these numbers.
- use decimal notation for tenths, hundredths and thousandths.

Learning objectives

Objective 1: Partition decimals with up to three places.

Learning outcomes

The children will be able to:
- partition numbers into tens, units, tenths, hundredths and thousandths

Success criteria

The children have a **secure** level of attainment in relation to Objective 1 if the following question can be answered with a 'yes'.

Can the children...
... complete the activities on the Assessment sheet accurately and confidently?

Administering the assessment

Ensure that the children understand the task and help them read the instructions if necessary. The ability to partition numbers is vitally important to the children's understanding of the number system. Watch their work carefully ensuring that they are able to complete the activity confidently to achieve the answers shown below. Discuss the answers with them, checking that they appreciate the position value of each digit e.g. do they understand that 0.103 consists of 1 tenth and 3 thousandths?

(This assessment will also provide evidence for assessing strand 1, Using and applying mathematics: Represent and interpret sequences, patterns and relationships involving numbers; Explain reasoning and conclusions, using words, symbols or diagrams as appropriate.)

Answers:

$2.9 = 2 + 0.9$
$3.75 = 3 + 0.7 + 0.05$
$14.2 = 10 + 4 + 0.2$
$1.465 = 1 + 0.4 + 0.06 + 0.005$
$0.92 = 0.9 + 0.02$
$0.736 = 0.7 + 0.03 + 0.006$
$0.054 = 0.05 + 0.004$
$0.103 = 0.1 + 0.003$
$5.08 = 5 + 0.08$
$24.006 = 20 + 4 + 0.006$

Andrew Brodie: Ten Minute Maths Assessments ages 10–11 © A&C Black 2009

Partition decimals with up to three places

Name

Date

The number 3.456 can be partitioned like this:

3.456 = 3 + 0.4 + 0.05 + 0.006

Partition the following numbers in the same way:

2.9 = --

3.75 = --

14.2 = --

1.465 = --

0.92 = --

0.736 = --

0.054 = --

0.103 = --

5.08 = --

24.006 = --

I can partition decimals with up to three places.

Round decimals with up to three places

Building on previous learning

Before starting this unit check that the children can already:
- read, write and order whole numbers to at least 1000 and position them on a number line.
- partition whole numbers and decimals with up to two places.
- round whole numbers and decimals with up to two places.

Learning objectives

Objective 1: Round whole numbers and decimals with up to three places to the nearest 10, 1, $\frac{1}{10}$ or $\frac{1}{100}$.

Learning outcomes

The children will be able to:
- explain what each digit represents in whole numbers and decimals with up to three places.
- round up or down whole numbers and decimals with up to three places to the nearest 10, 1, $\frac{1}{10}$ or $\frac{1}{100}$.

Success criteria

The children have a **secure** level of attainment in relation to Objective 1 if the following questions can be answered with a 'yes'.

Can the children recognise that numbers such as...
... 28.4, 6.9, 2.48 can be rounded up to the nearest multiple of 10, 1 or $\frac{1}{10}$ respectively, to give an approximation?
... 32.9, 12.3, 3.61 can be rounded down to the nearest multiple of 10, 1 or $\frac{1}{10}$ respectively, to give an approximation?
... 45, 7.5, 4.65 can be rounded up to the nearest multiple of 10, 1 or $\frac{1}{10}$ respectively to give an approximation?

Administering the assessment

Ideally the children should work in a small group with an adult. Ensure that every child understands the tasks. The children need to be aware that, when rounding to the nearest 10, the *units* digit is more important than the *tenths* digit and that, when rounding to the nearest 1, the *tenths* digit is more important than the *hundredths* digit, etc. They will also need to know that we always round up from multiples of 5 when rounding to the nearest 10, from multiples of 0.5 when rounding to the nearest 1, from multiples of 0.05 when rounding to the nearest $\frac{1}{10}$ and from multiples of 0.005 when rounding to the nearest $\frac{1}{100}$.

(This assessment will also provide evidence for assessing strand 1, Using and applying mathematics: Represent and interpret sequences, patterns and relationships involving numbers; Explain reasoning and conclusions, using words, symbols or diagrams as appropriate.)

Answers:
30   210   40   60   80
7   16   83   100   24
0.2   0.8   0.4   8.6   14.4
5.64   14.21   3.63   0.07   0.85

Round decimals with up to three places

Name

Date

Round these numbers to the nearest ten.

27 — to the nearest ten →

214 — to the nearest ten →

35.8 — to the nearest ten →

63.2 — to the nearest ten →

75 — to the nearest ten →

Round these numbers to the nearest whole number.

7.4 — to the nearest whole number →

15.7 — to the nearest whole number →

82.9 — to the nearest whole number →

100.2 — to the nearest whole number →

23.5 — to the nearest whole number →

Round these numbers to the nearest tenth.

0.19 — to the nearest tenth →

0.76 — to the nearest tenth →

0.43 — to the nearest tenth →

8.62 — to the nearest tenth →

14.38 — to the nearest tenth →

Round these numbers to the nearest hundredth.

5.639 — to the nearest hundredth →

14.207 — to the nearest hundredth →

3.628 — to the nearest hundredth →

0.072 — to the nearest hundredth →

0.846 — to the nearest hundredth →

I can round numbers to the nearest ten, whole number, tenth or hundredth.

Order decimals with up to three places

Building on previous learning

Before starting this unit check that the children can already:

- read, write and order whole numbers to at least 1000 and position them on a number line.
- partition or round whole numbers and decimals with up to two places.
- order whole numbers and decimals with up to two places.

Learning objectives

Objective 1: Order decimals with up to three places.

Learning outcomes

The children will be able to:

- explain what each digit represents in whole numbers and decimals with up to three places.
- write sets of whole numbers and decimals with up to three places in order.
- create whole numbers and decimals with up to three places from separate digits by following given criteria.

Success criteria

The children have a **secure** level of attainment in relation to Objective 1 if the following questions can be answered with a 'yes'.

Can the children...

... write the sets of numbers shown on the Assessment sheet in order?

... create the largest possible or smallest possible number incorporating two or three decimal places from the digits provided on the Assessment sheet?

Administering the assessment

Ideally the children should work in a small group with an adult. You may decide to use the opportunity to also assess pupils' knowledge and skills in rounding the numbers shown to the nearest 10, 1, $\frac{1}{10}$ or $\frac{1}{100}$. Encourage the pupils to discuss the sheet, explaining the place values of the digits in the numbers. When you are confident that they are ready, allow them to complete the written tasks.

(This assessment will also provide evidence for assessing strand 1, Using and applying mathematics: Represent and interpret sequences, patterns and relationships involving numbers; Explain reasoning and conclusions, using words, symbols or diagrams as appropriate; Suggest, plan and develop lines of enquiry; collect organise and represent information, interpret results and review methods; identify and answer related questions.)

Answers:			
0.297	2.97	29.7	297
0.56	0.65	5.6	6.5
1.345	3.154	4.135	5.431
0.368	0.386	0.638	0.836
87.43	34.78	8.743	3.478

Order decimals with up to three places

Name _____

Date _____

Write each set of numbers in order, starting with the smallest

2.97   29.7   297   0.297

----------------   ----------------   ----------------   ----------------

0.65   0.56   6.5   5.6

----------------   ----------------   ----------------   ----------------

3.154   1.345   4.135   5.431

----------------   ----------------   ----------------   ----------------

0.638   0.836   0.368   0.386

----------------   ----------------   ----------------   ----------------

Look at the four digit cards.

| 7 | 4 | 8 | 3 |

Using each digit only once, write the
largest possible number that has two decimal places.   ----------------

Using each digit only once, write the
smallest possible number that has two decimal places.   ----------------

Using each digit only once, write the
largest possible number that has three decimal places.   ----------------

Using each digit only once, write the
smallest possible number that has three decimal places.   ----------------

I can write numbers, including decimals with up to three places, in order.

Andrew Brodie: Ten Minute Maths Assessments ages 10–11 © A&C Black 2009

Position decimals with up to three places on the number line

Building on previous learning

Before starting this unit check that the children can already:

- read, write and order whole numbers to at least 1000 and position them on a number line.
- partition or round whole numbers and decimals with up to two places.
- order whole numbers and decimals with up to two places.
- order decimals with up to three places.

Learning objectives

Objective 1: Position decimals with up to three places on the number line.

Learning outcomes

The children will be able to:

- use their knowledge of place value to find the approximate positions of decimals with up to three places on a number line.

Success criteria

The children will have a **secure** level of attainment in relation to Objective 1 if the following questions can be answered with a 'yes'.

Can the children...

... write the numbers shown on the Assessment sheet in approximately the correct places on the number line?

... position the number 0.256 appropriately between 0.25 and 0.3?

... position the number 1.755 appropriately between 1.75 and 1.8?

Administering the assessment

Ideally the children should work in a small group with an adult. Encourage the pupils to discuss the Assessment sheet, explaining the place values of the digits in the numbers. The number line has very few markings and the pupils will need to have secure understanding of place value to position the numbers appropriately. They do not need to be totally accurate but they do need to position the numbers relative to each other.

(This assessment will also provide evidence for assessing strand 1, Using and applying mathematics: Represent and interpret sequences, patterns and relationships involving numbers; Explain reasoning and conclusions, using words, symbols or diagrams as appropriate; Suggest, plan and develop lines of enquiry; collect organise and represent information, interpret results and review methods; identify and answer related questions.)

Answers:

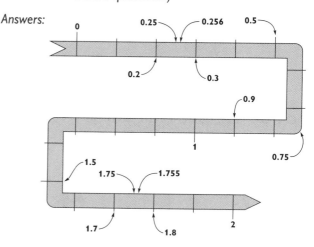

Position decimals with up to three places on the number line

Name

Date

Use your own skill and judgement to mark these numbers in approximately the correct places on the number line. The first three have been done for you.

~~0.5~~   ~~1.5~~   ~~0.75~~   0.25   0.3   0.9   1.7   0.256   0.2   1.8   1.75   1.755

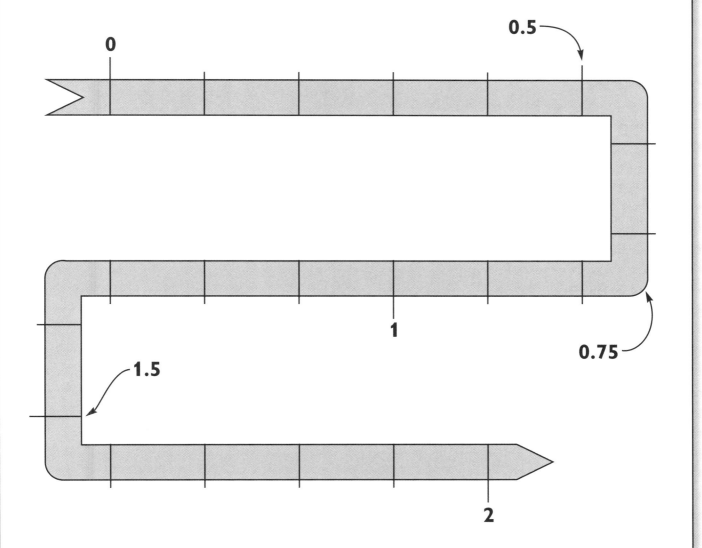

I can position decimals with up to three places on the number line.

Andrew Brodie: Ten Minute Maths Assessments ages 10–11 © A&C Black 2009

Express a larger whole number as a fraction of a smaller one

Building on previous learning

Before starting this unit check that the children can already:

- read and write proper fractions interpreting the denominator as the parts of a whole and the numerator as the number of parts.
- identify fractions shown on diagrams and match these to equivalent fractions on other diagrams.
- express a smaller number as a fraction of a larger one e.g. recognise that 5 out of 8 is $\frac{5}{8}$.

Learning objectives

Objective 1: Express a larger whole number as a fraction of a smaller one.

Learning outcomes

The children will be able to:

- express a larger number as a fraction of a smaller one e.g. recognise that 7 slices of a four-slice pizza represents $\frac{7}{4}$ or $1\frac{3}{4}$ pizzas.
- use appropriate vocabulary related to fractions: numerator, denominator, equivalent, proper fraction, improper fraction.

Success criteria

The children have a **secure** level of attainment in relation to Objective 1 if the following questions can be answered with a 'yes'.

Can the children...
... write the correct improper fraction for each picture?
... write the correct mixed number for each picture?
... explain the significance of each number in a fraction or mixed number?

Administering the assessment

Ideally the children should work in a small group with an adult. Encourage the pupils to discuss the pictures on the Assessment sheet, using appropriate mathematical vocabulary. Do they know that a number such as $\frac{7}{4}$ is called an improper fraction because the numerator is greater than the denominator? Do they know that $1\frac{3}{4}$ is called a mixed number because it is a mixture of a whole number and a fraction? Do they know that $1\frac{3}{4}$ is equivalent to $\frac{7}{4}$?

(This assessment will also provide evidence for assessing strand 1, Using and applying mathematics: Represent and interpret sequences, patterns and relationships involving numbers; Explain reasoning and conclusions, using words, symbols or diagrams as appropriate; Suggest, plan and develop lines of enquiry; collect organise and represent information, interpret results and review methods; identify and answer related questions.)

Answers: $\frac{7}{6}$ or $1\frac{1}{6}$ $\frac{7}{5}$ or $1\frac{2}{5}$ $\frac{5}{4}$ or $1\frac{1}{4}$

$\frac{11}{6}$ or $1\frac{5}{6}$ $\frac{11}{8}$ or $1\frac{3}{8}$

Express a larger whole number as a fraction of a smaller one

Name

Date

This is a whole pizza cut into four equal-sized pieces.

How many pizzas are shown in each picture below?
The first one is done for you.

$\frac{7}{4}$ or $1\frac{3}{4}$

I can express a larger whole number as a fraction of a smaller one.

Simplify fractions by cancelling common factors

Building on previous learning

Before starting this unit check that the children can already:

- read and write proper fractions interpreting the denominator as the parts of a whole and the numerator as the number of parts.
- identify fractions shown on diagrams and match these to equivalent fractions on other diagrams.
- express a smaller number as a fraction of a larger one e.g. recognise that 5 out of 8 is $\frac{5}{8}$.

Learning objectives

Objective 1: Simplify fractions by cancelling common factors.

Learning outcomes

The children will be able to:

- identify common factors for the numerator and denominator of each fraction.
- simplify the fractions by cancelling common factors.
- use appropriate vocabulary related to fractions: numerator, denominator, equivalent, simplify, cancel, reduced to.

Success criteria

The children have a **secure** level of attainment in relation to Objective 1 if the following questions can be answered with a 'yes'.

Can the children…

… identify common factors for the numerator and denominator of each fraction on the Assessment sheet?

… simplify the fractions on the Assessment sheet by cancelling common factors?

Administering the assessment

Ideally the children should work in a small group with an adult. Encourage the pupils to discuss the fractions on the Assessment sheet, using appropriate mathematical vocabulary. Do they know that some of the fractions can be simplified in different ways but ultimately will be reduced to the simplest form? E.g. $\frac{24}{30}$ could be reduced by dividing numerator and denominator by 2 to reach $\frac{12}{15}$, then dividing each by 3 to reach $\frac{4}{5}$ or it could be reduced by diving each by 6 to reach $\frac{4}{5}$.

(This assessment will also provide evidence for assessing strand 1, Using and applying mathematics: Represent and interpret sequences, patterns and relationships involving numbers; Explain reasoning and conclusions, using words, symbols or diagrams as appropriate; Suggest, plan and develop lines of enquiry; collect organise and represent information, interpret results and review methods; identify and answer related questions.)

Answers: $\frac{1}{2}$ $\quad$ $\frac{3}{4}$ $\quad$ $\frac{1}{4}$ $\quad$ $\frac{4}{5}$ $\quad$ $\frac{4}{5}$ $\quad$ $\frac{8}{9}$ $\quad$ $\frac{3}{5}$ $\quad$ $\frac{1}{4}$ $\quad$ $\frac{1}{5}$ $\quad$ $\frac{2}{5}$

Simplify fractions by cancelling common factors

Name

Date

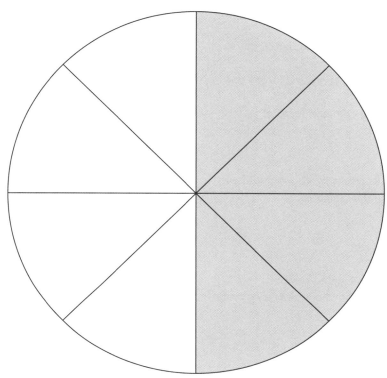

$\frac{4}{8}$ **is equivalent to** $\frac{1}{2}$

Simplify each of the fractions below:

$\frac{5}{10}$ is equivalent to _____

$\frac{16}{18}$ is equivalent to _____

$\frac{9}{12}$ is equivalent to _____

$\frac{12}{20}$ is equivalent to _____

$\frac{7}{28}$ is equivalent to _____

$\frac{25}{100}$ is equivalent to _____

$\frac{20}{25}$ is equivalent to _____

$\frac{20}{100}$ is equivalent to _____

$\frac{24}{30}$ is equivalent to _____

$\frac{40}{100}$ is equivalent to _____

I can simplify fractions by cancelling common factors.

Order a set of fractions by converting them to fractions with a common denominator

Building on previous learning

Before starting this unit check that the children can already:

- read and write proper fractions interpreting the denominator as the parts of a whole and the numerator as the number of parts.
- identify fractions shown on diagrams and match these to equivalent fractions on other diagrams.
- express a smaller number as a fraction of a larger one e.g. recognise that 5 out of 8 is $\frac{5}{8}$.
- simplify fractions by cancelling common factors.

Learning objectives

Objective 1: Order a set of fractions by converting them to fractions with a common denominator.

Learning outcomes

The children will be able to:

- compare two fractions using inequality symbols.
- convert each set of fractions to fractions with a common denominator.
- arrange each set of fractions in order.

Success criteria

The children have a **secure** level of attainment in relation to Objective 1 if the following questions can be answered with a 'yes'.

Can the children…

… compare two fractions using inequality symbols appropriately?

… confidently convert fractions to fractions with a common denominator?

… arrange these fractions in order?

Administering the assessment

Ideally the children should work in a small group with an adult. Encourage the pupils to discuss the fractions on the Assessment sheet, using appropriate mathematical vocabulary. The focus of the assessment is whether the children can quickly and confidently convert fractions so that they have common denominators, then use this to put the fractions in order of size.

(This assessment will also provide evidence for assessing strand 1, Using and applying mathematics: Represent and interpret sequences, patterns and relationships involving numbers; Explain reasoning and conclusions, using words, symbols or diagrams as appropriate; Suggest, plan and develop lines of enquiry; collect organise and represent information, interpret results and review methods; identify and answer related questions; Tabulate systematically the information in a problem or puzzle; identify and record the steps or calculations needed to solve it, using symbols where appropriate; interpret solutions in the original context and check their accuracy.)

Answers: $\frac{1}{2} > \frac{1}{4}$ $\qquad$ $\frac{1}{4} < \frac{1}{3}$ $\qquad$ $\frac{1}{4} > \frac{1}{5}$

$\frac{1}{3} < \frac{2}{5}$ $\qquad$ $\frac{3}{4} < \frac{4}{5}$ $\qquad$ $\frac{3}{4} > \frac{2}{3}$

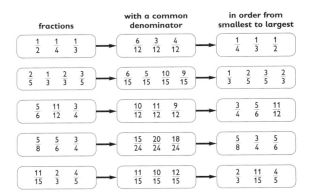

Andrew Brodie: Ten Minute Maths Assessments ages 10–11 © A&C Black 2009

Order a set of fractions by converting them to fractions with a common denominator

Name

Date

Look at each pair of fractions.
Write the correct symbol < or > in the box between them.

$\frac{1}{2}$ ◯ $\frac{1}{4}$ $\frac{1}{4}$ ◯ $\frac{1}{3}$ $\frac{1}{4}$ ◯ $\frac{1}{5}$ $\frac{1}{3}$ ◯ $\frac{2}{5}$ $\frac{3}{4}$ ◯ $\frac{4}{5}$ $\frac{3}{4}$ ◯ $\frac{2}{3}$

Convert each set of fractions to fractions with a common denominator.
Write the original fractions out again in the correct order, starting with the smallest. The first set has been done for you.

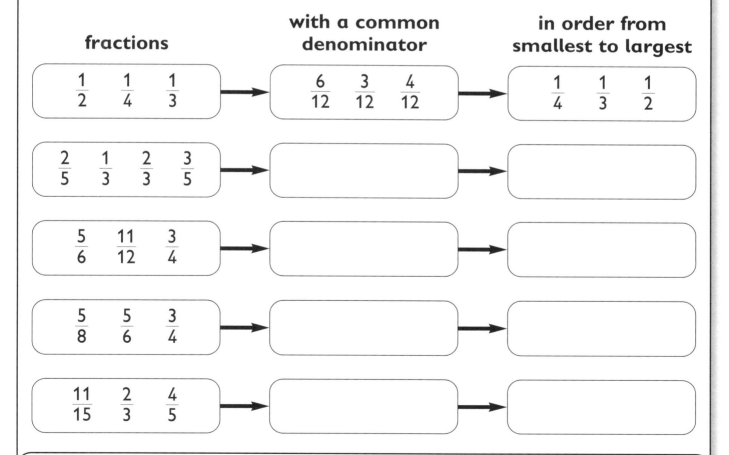

fractions			with a common denominator			in order from smallest to largest		
$\frac{1}{2}$	$\frac{1}{4}$	$\frac{1}{3}$	$\frac{6}{12}$	$\frac{3}{12}$	$\frac{4}{12}$	$\frac{1}{4}$	$\frac{1}{3}$	$\frac{1}{2}$
$\frac{2}{5}$	$\frac{1}{3}$	$\frac{2}{3}$ $\frac{3}{5}$						
$\frac{5}{6}$	$\frac{11}{12}$	$\frac{3}{4}$						
$\frac{5}{8}$	$\frac{5}{6}$	$\frac{3}{4}$						
$\frac{11}{15}$	$\frac{2}{3}$	$\frac{4}{5}$						

I can order a set of fractions by converting them to fractions with a common denominator.

Andrew Brodie: Ten Minute Maths Assessments ages 10–11 © A&C Black 2009

Express one quantity as a percentage of another

Building on previous learning

Before starting this unit check that the children can already:
- read and write proper fractions interpreting the denominator as the parts of a whole and the numerator as the number of parts.
- use decimal notation for tenths and hundredths.
- understand percentage as the number of parts in every 100.
- express tenths and hundredths as percentages.
- relate fractions to their decimal representations.

Learning objectives

Objective 1: Express one quantity as a percentage of another.

Learning outcomes

The children will be able to:
- express one quantity as a percentage of another.

Success criteria

The children have a **secure** level of attainment in relation to Objective 1 if the following questions can be answered with a 'yes'.

Can the children...
... express quantities out of 100, 10 or 1000 as a percentage?
... express quantities out of 50, 25 or 20 as a percentage?

Administering the assessment

Track 3 Ensure that the children understand the task and help them read the instructions if necessary. The assessment relies on the CD for a timed test where the children are given ten seconds to answer each question. This is the script for the CD if you decide to dictate the questions (the answers are provided after each question below).

I will say each of the first three questions twice then you will have five seconds to answer it.
Question 1: 38 of the 100 trees in an orchard are pear trees. What percentage are pear trees?   38%
Question 2: 57 children out of the total 100 children in a school are girls. What percentage of the pupils are girls?   57%
Question 3: 100 people were questioned in a survey about tea and coffee. 68 people said they prefer to drink tea. What percentage is this?   68%

I will say each of the next questions twice then you will have ten seconds to answer it.
Question 4: 7 out of 10 people say they drink three or more hot drinks per day. What percentage is this?   70%
Question 5: 7 out of 10 people say they drink three or more hot drinks per day. What percentage drink fewer than three hot drinks?   30%
Question 6: Express £9 as a percentage of £10   90%
Question 7: What is £2.50 as a percentage of £10?   25%
Question 8: What percentage of £10 is £8.50?   85%
Question 9: Express £600 as a percentage of £1000.   60%
Question 10: 23 out of 50 pupils have black shoes on. What percentage are wearing black shoes?   46%
Question 11: 5 out of 20 people ride a bike to work. What percentage travel to work by bike?   25%
Question 12: Express £12 as a percentage of £25.   48%

(This assessment will also provide evidence for assessing strand 1, Using and applying mathematics: Solve multi-step problems, and problems involving fractions, decimals and percentages; Represent and interpret sequences, patterns and relationships involving numbers; Explain reasoning and conclusions, using words, symbols or diagrams as appropriate.)

Andrew Brodie: Ten Minute Maths Assessments ages 10–11 © A&C Black 2009

Express one quantity as a percentage of another

Name

Date

Listen to the CD or your teacher. Write the percentages.

1.

2.

3.

4.

5.

6.

7.

8.

9.

10.

11.

12.

I can express one quantity as a percentage of another.

Andrew Brodie: Ten Minute Maths Assessments ages 10–11 © A&C Black 2009

Find equivalent percentages, decimals and fractions

Building on previous learning

Before starting this unit check that the children can already:

- read and write proper fractions interpreting the denominator as the parts of a whole and the numerator as the number of parts.
- use decimal notation for tenths and hundredths.
- understand percentage as the number of parts in every 100.
- express tenths and hundredths as percentages.
- relate fractions to their decimal representations.

Learning objectives

Objective 1: Find equivalent percentages, decimals and fractions.

Learning outcomes

The children will be able to:

- match fractions to equivalent decimals and decimals to equivalent percentages.

Success criteria

The children have a **secure** level of attainment in relation to Objective 1 if the following questions can be answered with a 'yes'.

Can the children...
... match each fraction to its equivalent decimal form?
... match each decimal to its equivalent percentage?

Administering the assessment

Ensure that the children understand the task and help them read the instructions if necessary. Discuss the example provided to check that the pupils understand that $\frac{1}{2}$ is equivalent to the decimal form 0.5 and they are both equivalent to 50%. Look carefully at their answers with them: some children are likely to match $\frac{1}{4}$ to 0.4, for example.

(This assessment will also provide evidence for assessing strand 1, Using and applying mathematics: Solve multi-step problems, and problems involving fractions, decimals and percentages; Represent and interpret sequences, patterns and relationships involving numbers; Explain reasoning and conclusions, using words, symbols or diagrams as appropriate.)

Answers:

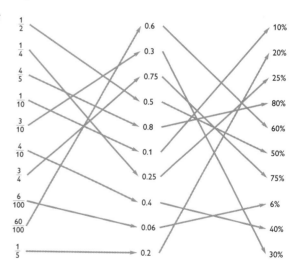

Andrew Brodie: Ten Minute Maths Assessments ages 10–11 © A&C Black 2009

Find equivalent percentages, decimals and fractions

Name

Date

Match the fractions, decimals and percentages.
The first one has been done for you.

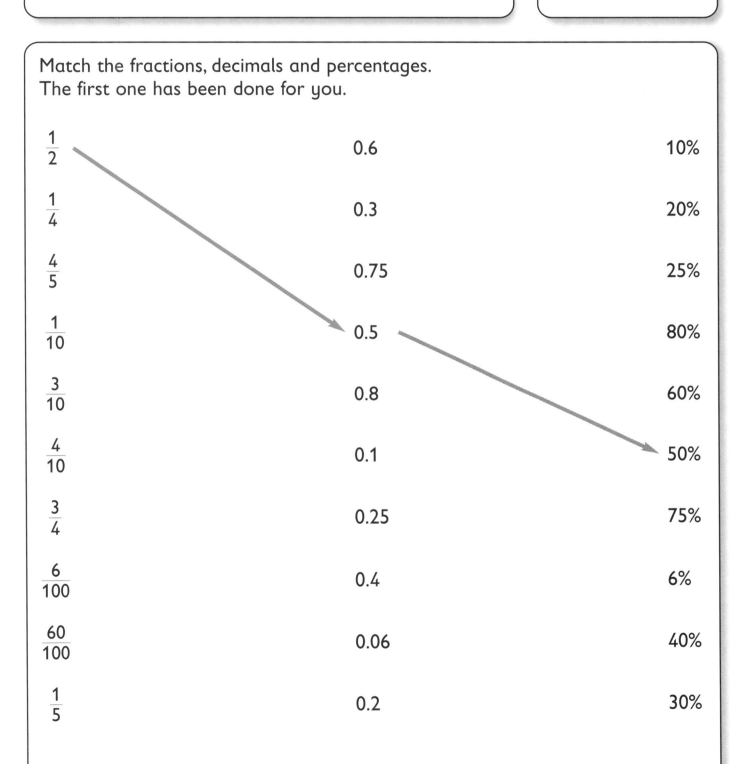

$\frac{1}{2}$	0.6	10%
$\frac{1}{4}$	0.3	20%
$\frac{4}{5}$	0.75	25%
$\frac{1}{10}$	0.5	80%
$\frac{3}{10}$	0.8	60%
$\frac{4}{10}$	0.1	50%
$\frac{3}{4}$	0.25	75%
$\frac{6}{100}$	0.4	6%
$\frac{60}{100}$	0.06	40%
$\frac{1}{5}$	0.2	30%

I can find equivalent percentages, decimals and fractions.

Andrew Brodie: Ten Minute Maths Assessments ages 10–11 © A&C Black 2009

Solve simple problems involving direct proportion by scaling quantities up or down

Building on previous learning

Before starting this unit check that the children can already:
- solve one-step and two-step problems involving numbers, money or measure.
- solve problems involving proportions of quantities.

Learning objectives

Objective 1: Solve simple problems involving direct proportion by scaling quantities up or down.

Learning outcomes

The children will be able to:
- solve simple problems involving direct proportion by scaling quantities up or down.

Success criteria

The children have a **secure** level of attainment in relation to Objective 1 if the following question can be answered with a 'yes'.

Can the children…
… solve the problems on the Assessment sheet quickly and accurately?

Administering the assessment

Ensure that the children understand the task and help them read the questions if necessary. You may decide to discuss the first question as many children find this subject very difficult. Encourage them to draw pictures on the sheet to help them to visualise the problem if they need to.

(This assessment will also provide evidence for assessing strand 1, Using and applying mathematics: Solve multi-step problems, and problems involving fractions, decimals and percentages; choose and use appropriate calculation strategies at each stage; Tabulate systematically the information in a problem or puzzle; identify and record the steps or calculations needed to solve it, using symbols where appropriate; interpret solutions in the original context and check their accuracy; Represent and interpret sequences, patterns and relationships involving numbers; Explain reasoning and conclusions, using words, symbols or diagrams as appropriate.)

Answers: 1. 2 pots   2. 6 pots   3. 12 litres   4. 30 litres

Solve simple problems involving direct proportion by scaling quantities up or down

Name

Date

Pink paint can be made by mixing one pot of red paint with two pots of white paint.

Answer these questions about the paint.

1. How much red paint would you need to make a total of six pots of pink paint?

2. How much white paint would you need to make a total of nine pots of pink paint?

Orange drink is being prepared for a school party.
One litre of orange squash is mixed with water to make a total of five litres of orange drink.

Answer these questions about the orange squash.

3. How much water would be needed to make a total of fifteen litres of orange drink?

4. How much orange drink could be made altogether from water mixed with six litres of orange squash?

I can solve simple problems involving direct proportion by scaling quantities up or down.

Use multiplication facts from the 6 times table to derive related multiplication and division facts involving decimals

Building on previous learning

Before starting this unit check that the children can already:
- derive and recall multiplication facts for all tables up to 10 x 10.

Learning objectives

Objective 1: Recall multiplication facts for the 6 times table.

Objective 2: Use multiplication facts from the 6 times table to derive related multiplication and division facts involving decimals.

Learning outcomes

The children will be able to:
- recall multiplication facts for the 6 times table rapidly and confidently and use these facts to derive related multiplication and division facts.

Success criteria

The children have a **secure** level of attainment in relation to the Objective 1 if the following question can be answered with a 'yes'.

Can the children...

... respond quickly and accurately to the questions on the CD?

Administering the assessment

● Track 4 Ensure that the children understand the task. They should be able to answer the questions without the need to pause the CD as this assessment is concerned with rapid recall. This is the script for the CD if you decide to dictate the questions (the answers are provided after each question below).

I will say each of the questions twice then you will have five seconds to answer it.

Question 1: 0.4 times 6	2.4
Question 2: 0.7 times 6	4.2
Question 3: 0.9 times 6	5.4
Question 4: 0.5 times 6	3
Question 5: 0.1 times 6	0.6
Question 6: 0.8 times 6	4.8
Question 7: 0.2 times 6	1.2
Question 8: 0.6 times 6	3.6
Question 9: 0.3 times 6	1.8
Question 10: 4.8 divided by 6	0.8
Question 11: 3 divided by 6	0.5
Question 12: 1.8 divided by 6	0.3
Question 13: 5.4 divided by 6	0.9
Question 14: 3.6 divided by 6	0.6
Question 15: 0.6 divided by 6	0.1
Question 16: 2.4 divided by 6	0.4
Question 17: 1.2 divided by 6	0.2
Question 18: 4.2 divided by 6	0.7
Question 19: 7.2 divided by 6	1.2
Question 20: 9 divided by 6	1.5

Andrew Brodie: Ten Minute Maths Assessments ages 10–11 © A&C Black 2009

Use multiplication facts from the 6 times table to derive related multiplication and division facts involving decimals

Name

Date

Listen carefully to the CD or your teacher.
Write the answers to the questions in the boxes.

1.

2.

3.

4.

5.

6.

7.

8.

9.

10.

11.

12.

13.

14.

15.

16.

17.

18.

19.

20.

I can recall quickly the multiplication and division facts for the 6 times table.

I can use multiplication facts from the 6 times table to derive related multiplication and division facts involving decimals.

Use multiplication facts from the 7 times table to derive related multiplication and division facts involving decimals

Building on previous learning

Before starting this unit check that the children can already:
- derive and recall multiplication facts for all tables up to 10 x 10.

Learning objectives

Objective 1: Recall multiplication facts for the 7 times table.

Objective 2: Use multiplication facts from the 7 times table to derive related multiplication and division facts involving decimals.

Learning outcomes

The children will be able to:
- recall multiplication facts for the 7 times table rapidly and confidently and use these facts to derive related multiplication and division facts.

Success criteria

The children have a **secure** level of attainment in relation to Objective 1 if the following question can be answered with a 'yes'.

Can the children...

... respond quickly and accurately to the questions on the CD?

Administering the assessment

● **Track 5** Ensure that the children understand the task. They should be able to answer the questions without the need to pause the CD as this assessment is concerned with rapid recall. This is the script for the CD if you decide to dictate the questions (the answers are provided after each question below).

I will say each of the questions twice then you will have five seconds to answer it.

Question 1: 0.6 times 7	4.2
Question 2: 0.9 times 7	6.3
Question 3: 0.4 times 7	2.8
Question 4: 0.1 times 7	0.7
Question 5: 0.3 times 7	2.1
Question 6: 0.8 times 7	5.6
Question 7: 0.2 times 7	1.4
Question 8: 0.7 times 7	4.9
Question 9: 0.5 times 7	3.5
Question 10: 4.9 divided by 7	0.7
Question 11: 3.5 divided by 7	0.5
Question 12: 1.4 divided by 7	0.2
Question 13: 5.6 divided by 7	0.8
Question 14: 0.7 divided by 7	0.1
Question 15: 4.2 divided by 7	0.6
Question 16: 6.3 divided by 7	0.9
Question 17: 2.1 divided by 7	0.3
Question 18: 2.8 divided by 7	0.4
Question 19: 7.7 divided by 7	1.1
Question 20: 8.4 divided by 7	1.2

Andrew Brodie: Ten Minute Maths Assessments ages 10–11 © A&C Black 2009

Use multiplication facts from the 7 times table to derive related multiplication and division facts involving decimals

Name

Date

Listen carefully to the CD or your teacher.
Write the answers to the questions in the boxes.

1.

2.

3.

4.

5.

6.

7.

8.

9.

10.

11.

12.

13.

14.

15.

16.

17.

18.

19.

20.

I can recall quickly the multiplication and division facts for the 7 times table.

I can use multiplication facts from the 7 times table to derive related multiplication and division facts involving decimals.

Use multiplication facts from the 8 times table to derive related multiplication and division facts involving decimals

Building on previous learning

Before starting this unit check that the children can already:
- derive and recall multiplication facts for all tables up to 10 x 10.

Learning objectives

Objective 1: Recall multiplication facts for the 8 times table.

Objective 2: Use multiplication facts from the 8 times table to derive related multiplication and division facts involving decimals.

Learning outcomes

The children will be able to:
- recall multiplication facts for the 8 times table rapidly and confidently and use these facts to derive related multiplication and division facts.

Success criteria

The children have a **secure** level of attainment in relation to Obejctive 1 and 2 if the following question can be answered with a 'yes'.

Can the children...
... respond quickly and accurately to the questions on the CD?

Administering the assessment

🔘 Track 6   Ensure that the children understand the task. They should be able to answer the questions without the need to pause the CD as this assessment is concerned with rapid recall. This is the script for the CD if you decide to dictate the questions (the answers are provided after each question below).

I will say each of the questions twice then you will have five seconds to answer it.

Question 1: 0.5 times 8	4
Question 2: 0.9 times 8	7.2
Question 3: 0.1 times 8	0.8
Question 4: 0.6 times 8	4.8
Question 5: 0.3 times 8	2.4
Question 6: 0.2 times 8	1.6
Question 7: 0.7 times 8	5.6
Question 8: 0.4 times 8	3.2
Question 9: 0.8 times 8	6.4
Question 10: 1.6 divided by 8	0.2
Question 11: 3.2 divided by 8	0.4
Question 12: 5.6 divided by 8	0.7
Question 13: 7.2 divided by 8	0.9
Question 14: 0.8 divided by 8	0.1
Question 15: 4 divided by 8	0.5
Question 16: 2.4 divided by 8	0.3
Question 17: 4.8 divided by 8	0.6
Question 18: 6.4 divided by 8	0.8
Question 19: 8.8 divided by 8	1.1
Question 20: 10.4 divided by 8	1.3

Use multiplication facts from the 8 times table to derive related multiplication and division facts involving decimals

Name

Date

Listen carefully to the CD or your teacher.
Write the answers to the questions in the boxes.

1.

2.

3.

4.

5.

6.

7.

8.

9.

10.

11.

12.

13.

14.

15.

16.

17.

18.

19.

20.

I can recall quickly the multiplication and division facts for the 8 times table.

I can use multiplication facts from the 8 times table to derive related multiplication and division facts involving decimals.

Use multiplication facts from the 9 times table to derive related multiplication and division facts involving decimals

Building on previous learning

Before starting this unit check that the children can already:

- derive and recall multiplication facts for all tables up to 10 × 10.

Learning objectives

Objective 1: Recall multiplication facts for the 9 times table.

Objective 2: Use multiplication facts from the 9 times table to derive related multiplication and division facts involving decimals.

Learning outcomes

The children will be able to:

- recall multiplication facts for the 9 times table rapidly and confidently and use these facts to derive related multiplication and division facts.

Success criteria

The children have a **secure** level of attainment in relation to Objective 1 and 2 if the following question can be answered with a 'yes'.

Can the children...

... respond quickly and accurately to the questions on the CD?

Administering the assessment

Track 7 Ensure that the children understand the task. They should be able to answer the questions without the need to pause the CD as this assessment is concerned with rapid recall. This is the script for the CD if you decide to dictate the questions (the answers are provided after each question below).

I will say each of the questions twice then you will have five seconds to answer it.

Question 1: 0.1 times 9	0.9
Question 2: 0.9 times 9	8.1
Question 3: 0.3 times 9	2.7
Question 4: 0.6 times 9	5.4
Question 5: 0.2 times 9	1.8
Question 6: 0.7 times 9	6.3
Question 7: 0.4 times 9	3.6
Question 8: 0.5 times 9	4.5
Question 9: 0.8 times 9	7.2
Question 10: 1.8 divided by 9	0.2
Question 11: 4.5 divided by 9	0.5
Question 12: 6.3 divided by 9	0.7
Question 13: 0.9 divided by 9	0.1
Question 14: 3.6 divided by 9	0.4
Question 15: 5.4 divided by 9	0.6
Question 16: 7.2 divided by 9	0.8
Question 17: 8.1 divided by 9	0.9
Question 18: 2.7 divided by 9	0.3
Question 19: 10.8 divided by 9	1.2
Question 20: 14.4 divided by 9	1.6

Use multiplication facts from the 9 times table to derive related multiplication and division facts involving decimals

Name

Date

Listen carefully to the CD or your teacher.
Write the answers to the questions in the boxes.

1.

2.

3.

4.

5.

6.

7.

8.

9.

10.

11.

12.

13.

14.

15.

16.

17.

18.

19.

20.

I can recall quickly the multiplication and division facts for the
9 times table.

I can use multiplication facts from the 9 times table to derive
related multiplication and division facts involving decimals.

Use knowledge of multiplication facts to derive quickly squares of numbers to 12 x 12 and the corresponding squares of multiples of 10

Building on previous learning

Before starting this unit check that the children can already:
- derive and recall multiplication facts for all tables up to 10 x 10.

Learning objectives

Objective 1: Use knowledge of multiplication facts to derive quickly squares of numbers to 12 x 12 and the corresponding squares of multiples of 10.

Learning outcomes

The children will be able to:
- derive quickly squares of numbers to 12 x 1.
- derive quickly the corresponding squares of multiples of 10.

Success criteria

The children have a **secure** level of attainment in relation to Objective 1 if the following question can be answered with a 'yes'.

Can the children…
… respond quickly and accurately to the questions on the CD?

Administering the assessment

🔘 Track 8   Ensure that the children understand the task. If you feel that they need extra time you could pause the CD for some of the questions. This is the script for the CD if you decide to dictate the questions (the answers are provided after each question below).

I will say each of the questions twice then you will have five seconds to answer it.

Question 1: 3 squared	9
Question 2: 7 squared	49
Question 3: 1 squared	1
Question 4: 6 squared	36
Question 5: 10 squared	100
Question 6: 8 squared	64
Question 7: 4 squared	16
Question 8: 2 squared	4
Question 9: 5 squared	25
Question 10: 9 squared	81
Question 11: 30 squared	900
Question 12: 70 squared	4900
Question 13: 20 squared	400
Question 14: 80 squared	6400
Question 15: 50 squared	2500
Question 16: 90 squared	8100
Question 17: 40 squared	1600
Question 18: 60 squared	3600
Question 19: 11 squared	121
Question 20: 12 squared	144

Andrew Brodie: Ten Minute Maths Assessments ages 10–11 © A&C Black 2009

Use knowledge of multiplication facts to derive quickly squares of numbers to 12 x 12

Name

Date

Listen carefully to the CD or your teacher.
Write the answers to the questions in the boxes.

1.

2.

3.

4.

5.

6.

7.

8.

9.

10.

11.

12.

13.

14.

15.

16.

17.

18.

19.

20.

I can derive quickly the squares of numbers to 12 x 12.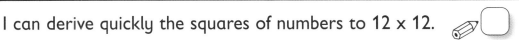

I can derive quickly the corresponding squares of multiples of 10.

Recognise that prime numbers have only two factors

Building on previous learning

Before starting this unit check that the children can already:
- derive and recall multiplication facts for all tables up to 10 x 1.
- identify pairs of factors of two-digit whole numbers.

Learning objectives

Objective 1: Recognise that prime numbers have only two factors.

Learning outcomes

The children will be able to:
- list the factors of any two-digit number.
- identify the prime numbers as numbers with only two factors.

Success criteria

The children have a **secure** level of attainment in relation to Objective 1 if the following questions can be answered with a 'yes'.

Can the children...
... find the factors of the numbers provided on the worksheet?
... identify the prime numbers?

Administering the assessment

Ensure that the children understand the task. You could discuss the first number with them.

(This assessment will also provide evidence for assessing strand 1, Using and applying mathematics: Tabulate systematically the information in a problem or puzzle; identify and record the steps or calculations needed to solve it, using symbols where appropriate; interpret solutions in the original context and check their accuracy; Suggest, plan and develop lines of enquiry; collect, organise and represent information, interpret results and review methods; identify and answer related questions; Represent and interpret sequences, patterns and relationships involving numbers and shapes; suggest and test hypotheses; construct and use simple expressions and formulae in words then symbols; Explain reasoning and conclusions, using words, symbols or diagrams as appropriate.)

Answers:	8:	1	8	2	4			
	12:	1	12	2	6	3	4	
	9:	1	9	3				
	11:	1	11					
	10:	1	10	2	5			
	7:	1	7					
	20:	1	20	2	10	4	5	
	19:	1	19					
	24:	1	24	2	12	3	8	4	6
	23:	1	23					
	11	7	19	23				

prime numbers

Recognise that prime numbers have only two factors

Name

Date

Look at each number.
Write the factors for each number in the boxes provided.

number	factors
8	⬜ ⬜ ⬜ ⬜
12	⬜ ⬜ ⬜ ⬜ ⬜ ⬜
9	⬜ ⬜ ⬜
11	⬜ ⬜
10	⬜ ⬜ ⬜ ⬜
7	⬜ ⬜
20	⬜ ⬜ ⬜ ⬜ ⬜ ⬜
19	⬜ ⬜
24	⬜ ⬜ ⬜ ⬜ ⬜ ⬜ ⬜ ⬜
23	⬜ ⬜

Which of the numbers have only two factors? ⬜ ⬜ ⬜ ⬜

What special name is given to these numbers? ------------------------------------

I can find factors of numbers. ✏️⬜

I can recognise prime numbers as they have only two factors. ✏️⬜

Andrew Brodie: Ten Minute Maths Assessments ages 10–11 © A&C Black 2009

Identify prime numbers less than 100

Building on previous learning

Before starting this unit check that the children can already:

- derive and recall multiplication facts for all tables up to 10 x 10.
- identify pairs of factors of two-digit whole numbers.

Learning objectives

Objective 1: Identify prime numbers less than 100.

Learning outcomes

The children will be able to:

- use the *Sieve of Eratostenes* to reveal the prime numbers.
- remember that prime numbers are numbers with only two factors.
- state the prime numbers less than 100.
- identify the only even prime number as 2.

Success criteria

The children have a **secure** level of attainment in relation to Objective 1 if the following questions can be answered with a 'yes'.

Can the children...

... list the prime numbers less than 100?

... explain that prime numbers have only two factors, themselves and one?

Administering the assessment

Ensure that the children understand the task. This method of finding the prime numbers less than 100 is called the *Sieve of Eratostenes*. Discuss the prime numbers with the children, encouraging them to realise that prime numbers don't appear in any multiplication tables apart from being the first multiplication fact of their own table i.e. 2 only appears in the 2 times table and is the first product.

(This assessment will also provide evidence for assessing strand 1, Using and applying mathematics: Tabulate systematically the information in a problem or puzzle; identify and record the steps or calculations needed to solve it, using symbols where appropriate; interpret solutions in the original context and check their accuracy; Suggest, plan and develop lines of enquiry; collect, organise and represent information, interpret results and review methods; identify and answer related questions; Represent and interpret sequences, patterns and relationships involving numbers and shapes; suggest and test hypotheses; construct and use simple expressions and formulae in words then symbols; Explain reasoning and conclusions, using words, symbols or diagrams as appropriate.)

Answers: *2 3 5 7 11 13 17 19 23 29 31 37 41 43 47 53 59 61 67 71 73 79 83 89 97*

The even prime number is 2.

Identify prime numbers less than 100

Name

Date

Use the hundred square to reveal the prime numbers less than 100.

Follow these steps:
Step 1: Shade the number 1 as it is not a prime number.
Step 2: Leave number 2 as it is a prime number but shade every other multiple of 2.
Step 3: Leave number 3 as it is a prime number but shade every other multiple of 3.
Step 4: Leave number 5 as it is a prime number but shade every other multiple of 5.
Step 5: Leave number 7 as it is a prime number but shade every other multiple of 7.

1	2	3	4	5	6	7	8	9	10
11	12	13	14	15	16	17	18	19	20
21	22	23	24	25	26	27	28	29	30
31	32	33	34	35	36	37	38	39	40
41	42	43	44	45	46	47	48	49	50
51	52	53	54	55	56	57	58	59	60
61	62	63	64	65	66	67	68	69	70
71	72	73	74	75	76	77	78	79	80
81	82	83	84	85	86	87	88	89	90
91	92	93	94	95	96	97	98	99	100

The prime numbers less than 100 are:

The only prime number that is even is:

I can identify prime numbers less than 100.

Calculate mentally with integers and decimals: U.t + U.t

Building on previous learning

Before starting this unit check that the children can already:
- derive and recall all addition facts for each number to 20.
- derive and recall sums and differences of multiples of 10.
- derive and recall number pairs that total 100.
- identify the doubles of two-digit numbers.
- add mentally pairs of two-digit whole numbers.
- use mental methods for adding whole numbers.

Learning objectives

Objective 1: Use mental methods for adding integers and decimals.

Learning outcomes

The children will be able to:
- use mental methods for an increasing range of additions.

Success criteria

The children have a **secure** level of attainment in relation to Objective 1 if the following question can be answered with a 'yes'.

Can the children...

... respond quickly and accurately to the questions on the CD?

Administering the assessment

Track 9 Ensure that the children understand the task. Watch their work carefully to check that they have appropriate strategies for the calculations. Simple jottings should be allowed but this assessment is of mental methods and children should not use formal written methods. A period of ten seconds is allowed for each question but you may need to pause the CD for some questions. This is the script for the CD if you decide to dictate the questions (the answers are provided after each question below).

I will say each of the questions twice then you will have ten seconds to answer it.

Question 1: 1.6 add 1.3	2.9
Question 2: 2.7 add 1.2	3.9
Question 3: 5.2 add 2.3	7.5
Question 4: 4.2 add 3.2	7.4
Question 5: 6.1 add 3.7	9.8
Question 6: 3.6 add 2.4	6
Question 7: 5.9 add 2.1	8
Question 8: 4.2 add 1.8	6
Question 9: 8.7 add 6.3	15
Question 10: 4.5 add 3.5	8
Question 11: 6.9 add 1.7	8.6
Question 12: 9.6 add 5.6	15.2
Question 13: 8.7 add 3.4	12.1
Question 14: 6.8 add 2.9	9.7
Question 15: 4.6 add 3.2	7.8
Question 16: 5.8 add 5.8	11.6
Question 17: 7.3 add 5.8	13.1
Question 18: 9.8 add 6.4	16.2
Question 19: 8.5 add 8.5	17
Question 20: 6.9 add 4.7	11.6

(This assessment will also provide evidence for assessing strand 1, Using and applying mathematics: Solve multi-step problems, and problems involving fractions, decimals and percentages; choose and use appropriate calculation strategies at each stage.)

Calculate mentally with integers and decimals: U.t + U.t

Name

Date

Listen carefully to the CD or your teacher.
Write the answers to the questions in the correct boxes.

1. [ ] | 1.6 1.3 | 11. [ ] | 6.9 1.7

2. [ ] | 2.7 1.2 | 12. [ ] | 9.6 5.6

3. [ ] | 5.2 2.3 | 13. [ ] | 8.7 3.4

4. [ ] | 4.2 3.2 | 14. [ ] | 6.8 2.9

5. [ ] | 6.1 3.7 | 15. [ ] | 4.6 3.2

6. [ ] | 3.6 2.4 | 16. [ ] | 5.8 5.8

7. [ ] | 5.9 2.1 | 17. [ ] | 7.3 5.8

8. [ ] | 4.2 1.8 | 18. [ ] | 9.8 6.4

9. [ ] | 8.7 6.3 | 19. [ ] | 8.5 8.5

10. [ ] | 4.5 3.5 | 20. [ ] | 6.9 4.7

I can add integers and decimals together mentally.

Calculate mentally with integers and decimals: U.t – U.t

Building on previous learning

Before starting this unit check that the children can already:
- derive and recall all addition facts for each number to 20.
- derive and recall sums and differences of multiples of 10.
- derive and recall number pairs that total 100.
- identify the doubles of two-digit numbers.
- subtract mentally pairs of two-digit whole numbers.
- use mental methods for subtracting whole numbers.

Learning objectives

Objective 1: Use mental methods for subtracting integers and decimals.

Learning outcomes

The children will be able to:
- use mental methods for an increasing range of subtractions.

Success criteria

The children have a **secure** level of attainment in relation to Objective 1 if the following question can be answered with a 'yes'.

Can the children...

... respond quickly and accurately to the questions on the CD?

Administering the assessment

🔘 **Track 10** Ensure that the children understand the task. Watch their work carefully to check if they have appropriate strategies for the calculations. Simple jottings should be allowed but this assessment is of mental methods and children should not use formal written methods. A period of ten seconds is allowed for each question but you may need to pause the CD for some of the questions. This is the script for the CD if you decide to dictate the questions (the answers are provided after each question below).

I will say each of the questions twice then you will have ten seconds to answer it.

Question 1: 3.8 minus 1.6	2.2
Question 2: 4.9 minus 2.1	2.8
Question 3: 9.6 minus 3.4	6.2
Question 4: 8.7 minus 5.2	3.5
Question 5: 5.9 minus 1.4	4.5
Question 6: 9.2 minus 2.1	7.1
Question 7: 7.6 minus 2.3	5.3
Question 8: 4.8 minus 1.1	3.7
Question 9: 8 minus 1.9	6.1
Question 10: 9 minus 2.8	6.2
Question 11: 7 minus 4.3	2.7
Question 12: 4 minus 1.8	2.2
Question 13: 5.1 minus 3.2	1.9
Question 14: 8.4 minus 3.9	4.5
Question 15: 7.4 minus 2.8	4.6
Question 16: 5.2 minus 1.9	3.3
Question 17: 9.5 minus 4.8	4.7
Question 18: 3.7 minus 0.9	2.8
Question 19: 6.4 minus 0.8	5.6
Question 20: 8.2 minus 1.6	6.6

(This assessment will also provide evidence for assessing strand 1, Using and applying mathematics: Solve multi-step problems, and problems involving fractions, decimals and percentages; choose and use appropriate calculation strategies at each stage.)

Andrew Brodie: Ten Minute Maths Assessments ages 10–11 © A&C Black 2009

Calculate mentally with integers and decimals: U.t – U.t

Name

Date

Listen carefully to the CD or your teacher.
Write the answers to the questions in the correct boxes.

1. [ ]   3.8 1.6   11. [ ]   7 4.3

2. [ ]   4.9 2.1   12. [ ]   4 1.8

3. [ ]   9.6 3.4   13. [ ]   5.1 3.2

4. [ ]   8.7 5.2   14. [ ]   8.4 3.9

5. [ ]   5.9 1.4   15. [ ]   7.4 2.8

6. [ ]   9.2 2.1   16. [ ]   5.2 1.9

7. [ ]   7.6 2.3   17. [ ]   9.5 4.8

8. [ ]   4.8 1.1   18. [ ]   3.7 0.9

9. [ ]   8 1.9   19. [ ]   6.4 0.8

10. [ ] 9 2.8   20. [ ]   8.2 1.6

I can subtract integers and decimals mentally.

Andrew Brodie: Ten Minute Maths Assessments ages 10–11 © A&C Black 2009

Calculate mentally with integers: TU x U

Building on previous learning

Before starting this unit check that the children can already:
- recall quickly multiplication facts up to 10 x 10 and derive the corresponding division facts.
- use mental methods for multiplying whole numbers.

Learning objectives

Objective 1: Use mental methods for multiplying two digit integers by one-digit integers.

Learning outcomes

The children will be able to:
- use mental methods for an increasing range of multiplications.

Success criteria

The children have a **secure** level of attainment in relation to Objective 1 if the following question can be answered with a 'yes'.

Can the children...
... respond quickly and accurately to the questions on the CD?

Administering the assessment

⬤ Track 11   Ensure that the children understand the task. Watch their work carefully to check if they have appropriate strategies for the calculations. Simple jottings should be allowed but this assessment is of mental methods and children should not use formal written methods. A period of ten seconds is allowed for each question but you may need to pause the CD for some of the questions. This is the script for the CD if you decide to dictate the questions (answers are provided after each question below.)

I will say each of the questions twice then you will have ten seconds to answer it.

Question 1: 17 times 3	*51*
Question 2: 12 times 7	*84*
Question 3: 19 times 4	*76*
Question 4: 16 times 5	*90*
Question 5: 18 times 8	*144*
Question 6: 13 times 9	*117*
Question 7: 14 times 6	*84*
Question 8: 17 times 8	*136*
Question 9: 15 times 5	*75*
Question 10: 16 times 9	*144*
Question 11: 21 times 4	*84*
Question 12: 25 times 6	*150*
Question 13: 32 times 7	*224*
Question 14: 25 times 9	*225*
Question 15: 41 times 4	*164*
Question 16: 53 times 6	*318*
Question 17: 67 times 5	*335*
Question 18: 48 times 3	*144*
Question 19: 24 times 6	*144*
Question 20: 25 times 8	*200*

(This assessment will also provide evidence for assessing strand 1, Using and applying mathematics: Solve multi-step problems, and problems involving fractions, decimals and percentages; choose and use appropriate calculation strategies at each stage.)

Calculate mentally with integers: TU x U

Name

Date

Listen carefully to the CD or your teacher.
Write the answers to the questions in the correct boxes.

1. | 17 3

2. | 12 7

3. | 19 4

4. | 16 5

5. | 18 8

6. | 13 9

7. | 14 6

8. | 17 8

9. | 15 5

10. | 16 9

11. | 21 4

12. | 25 6

13. | 32 7

14. | 25 9

15. | 41 4

16. | 53 6

17. | 67 5

18. | 48 3

19. | 24 6

20. | 25 8

I can multiply two digit integers by one-digit integers mentally.

Andrew Brodie: Ten Minute Maths Assessments ages 10–11 © A&C Black 2009

Calculate mentally with integers: TU ÷ U

Building on previous learning

Before starting this unit check that the children can already:

- recall quickly multiplication facts up to 10 x 10 and derive the corresponding division facts.
- use mental methods for multiplying and dividing whole numbers.

Learning objectives

Objective 1: Use mental methods for dividing two digit integers by one-digit integers.

Learning outcomes

The children will be able to:

- use mental methods for an increasing range of divisions.

Success criteria

The children have a **secure** level of attainment in relation to Objective 1 if the following question can be answered with a 'yes'.

Can the children...

... respond quickly and accurately to the questions on the CD?

Administering the assessment

🔘 **Track 12** Ensure that the children understand the task. Watch their work carefully to check if they have appropriate strategies for the calculations. Simple jottings should be allowed but this assessment is of mental methods and children should not use formal written methods. A period of ten seconds is allowed for each question but you may need to pause the CD for some of the questions. This is the script for the CD if you decide to dictate the questions (the answers are provided after each question below).

I will say each of the questions twice then you will have ten seconds to answer it.

Question 1: 51 divided by 3	17
Question 2: 88 divided by 4	22
Question 3: 78 divided by 6	13
Question 4: 52 divided by 4	13
Question 5: 90 divided by 6	15
Question 6: 57 divided by 3	19
Question 7: 69 divided by 3	23
Question 8: 91 divided by 7	13
Question 9: 84 divided by 6	14
Question 10: 85 divided by 5	17
Question 11: 95 divided by 5	19
Question 12: 90 divided by 2	45
Question 13: 76 divided by 2	38
Question 14: 92 divided by 4	23
Question 15: 99 divided by 3	33
Question 16: 81 divided by 3	27
Question 17: 70 divided by 5	14
Question 18: 96 divided by 8	12
Question 19: 96 divided by 4	24
Question 20: 98 divided by 7	14

(This assessment will also provide evidence for assessing strand 1, Using and applying mathematics: Solve multi-step problems, and problems involving fractions, decimals and percentages; choose and use appropriate calculation strategies at each stage.)

Calculate mentally with integers: TU ÷ U

Name

Date

Listen carefully to the CD or your teacher.
Write the answers to the questions in the correct boxes.

1.	51 3	**11.**	95 5
2.	88 4	**12.**	90 2
3.	78 6	**13.**	76 2
4.	52 4	**14.**	92 4
5.	90 6	**15.**	99 3
6.	57 3	**16.**	81 3
7.	69 3	**17.**	70 5
8.	91 7	**18.**	96 8
9.	84 6	**19.**	96 4
10.	85 5	**20.**	98 7

I can divide two digit integers by one-digit integers mentally.

Andrew Brodie: Ten Minute Maths Assessments ages 10–11 © A&C Black 2009

Calculate mentally with integers: U.t x U

Building on previous learning

Before starting this unit check that the children can already:
- recall quickly multiplication facts up to 10 x 10 and derive the corresponding division facts.
- use mental methods for multiplying whole numbers, including two-digit numbers by one-digit numbers.

Learning objectives

Objective 1: Use mental methods for multiplying numbers with decimals to one place by one-digit integers.

Learning outcomes

The children will be able to:
- use mental methods for an increasing range of multiplications, including multiplying numbers with decimals to one place by one-digit integers.

Success criteria

The children have a **secure** level of attainment in relation to Objective 1 if the following question can be answered with a 'yes'.

Can the children...
... respond quickly and accurately to the questions on the CD?

Administering the assessment

Track 13 Ensure that the children understand the task. Watch their work carefully to check if they have appropriate strategies for the calculations. Simple jottings should be allowed but this assessment is of mental methods and children should not use formal written methods. A period of ten seconds is allowed for each question but you may need to pause the CD for some of the questions. This is the script for the CD if you decide to dictate the questions (the answers are provided after each question below).

I will say each of the questions twice then you will have ten seconds to answer it.

Question 1: 1.2 times 3	3.6
Question 2: 2.5 times 2	5
Question 3: 4.7 times 3	14.1
Question 4: 5.2 times 2	10.4
Question 5: 1.8 times 4	7.2
Question 6: 1.5 times 3	4.5
Question 7: 2.5 times 6	15
Question 8: 3.5 times 4	14
Question 9: 2.9 times 3	8.7
Question 10: 1.6 times 4	6.4
Question 11: 3.2 times 5	16
Question 12: 2.4 times 4	9.6
Question 13: 1.9 times 5	9.5
Question 14: 2.7 times 3	8.1
Question 15: 7.5 times 4	30
Question 16: 8.2 times 6	49.2
Question 17: 9.3 times 7	65.1
Question 18: 4.6 times 6	27.6
Question 19: 5.5 times 5	27.5
Question 20: 6.5 times 8	52

(This assessment will also provide evidence for assessing strand 1, Using and applying mathematics: Solve multi-step problems, and problems involving fractions, decimals and percentages; choose and use appropriate calculation strategies at each stage.)

Calculate mentally with integers: U.t x U

Name

Date

Listen carefully to the CD or your teacher.
Write the answers to the questions in the correct boxes.

1. ( ) 1.2 3

2. ( ) 2.5 2

3. ( ) 4.7 3

4. ( ) 5.2 2

5. ( ) 1.8 4

6. ( ) 1.5 3

7. ( ) 2.5 6

8. ( ) 3.5 4

9. ( ) 2.9 3

10. ( ) 1.6 4

11. ( ) 3.2 5

12. ( ) 2.4 4

13. ( ) 1.9 5

14. ( ) 2.7 3

15. ( ) 7.5 4

16. ( ) 8.2 6

17. ( ) 9.3 7

18. ( ) 4.6 6

19. ( ) 5.5 5

20. ( ) 6.5 8

I can multiply numbers with decimals to one place by one-digit integers mentally.

Calculate mentally with integers: U.t ÷ U

Building on previous learning

Before starting this unit check that the children can already:
- recall quickly multiplication facts up to 10 x 10 and derive the corresponding division facts.
- use multiplication facts to 10 x 10 to derive division facts involving decimals.

Learning objectives

Objective 1: Use mental methods for dividing numbers with decimals to one place by one-digit integers.

Learning outcomes

The children will be able to:
- use mental methods for an increasing range of divisions, including dividing numbers with decimals to one place by one-digit integers.

Success criteria

The children have a **secure** level of attainment in relation to Objective 1 if the following question can be answered with a 'yes'.

Can the children...
... respond quickly and accurately to the questions on the CD?

Administering the assessment

● **Track 14** Ensure that the children understand the task. Watch their work carefully to check if they have appropriate strategies for the calculations. Simple jottings should be allowed but this assessment is of mental methods and children should not use formal written methods. A period of ten seconds is allowed for each question but you may need to pause the CD for some of the questions. This is the script for the CD if you decide to dictate the questions (the answers are provided after each question below).

I will say each of the questions twice then you will have ten seconds to answer it.

Question 1: 4.8 divided by 3	1.6
Question 2: 6.3 divided by 9	0.7
Question 3: 9.6 divided by 4	2.4
Question 4: 7.5 divided by 5	1.5
Question 5: 5.2 divided by 4	1.3
Question 6: 7.2 divided by 8	0.9
Question 7: 6.4 divided by 4	1.6
Question 8: 8.8 divided by 4	2.2
Question 9: 9.1 divided by 7	1.3
Question 10: 7.8 divided by 6	1.3
Question 11: 7.2 divided by 9	0.8
Question 12: 6.5 divided by 5	1.3
Question 13: 8.1 divided by 9	0.9
Question 14: 9.6 divided by 8	1.2
Question 15: 8.4 divided by 7	1.2
Question 16: 8.4 divided by 3	2.8
Question 17: 8.4 divided by 6	1.4
Question 18: 8.4 divided by 2	4.2
Question 19: 8.4 divided by 4	2.1
Question 20: 8.8 divided by 8	1.1

(This assessment will also provide evidence for assessing strand 1, Using and applying mathematics: Solve multi-step problems, and problems involving fractions, decimals and percentages; choose and use appropriate calculation strategies at each stage.)

Calculate mentally with integers: U.t ÷ U

Name

Date

Listen carefully to the CD or your teacher.
Write the answers to the questions in the correct boxes.

1. ( ) (4.8 3)

2. ( ) (6.3 9)

3. ( ) (9.6 4)

4. ( ) (7.5 5)

5. ( ) (5.2 4)

6. ( ) (7.2 8)

7. ( ) (6.4 4)

8. ( ) (8.8 4)

9. ( ) (9.1 7)

10. ( ) (7.8 6)

11. ( ) (7.2 9)

12. ( ) (6.5 5)

13. ( ) (8.1 9)

14. ( ) (9.6 8)

15. ( ) (8.4 7)

16. ( ) (8.4 3)

17. ( ) (8.4 6)

18. ( ) (8.4 2)

19. ( ) (8.4 4)

20. ( ) (8.8 8)

I can divide numbers with decimals to one place by one-digit integers mentally.

Use efficient written methods to add integers and decimals

Building on previous learning

Before starting this unit check that the children can already:
- derive and recall all addition facts for each number to 20.
- derive and recall sums and differences of multiples of 10.
- derive and recall number pairs that total 100.
- identify the doubles of two-digit numbers and derive the corresponding halves.
- develop and use written methods to record, support or explain addition of two-digit and three-digit numbers.
- use mental methods for adding integers and decimals.

Learning objectives

Objective 1: Use efficient written methods to add integers and decimals.

Learning outcomes

The children will be able to:
- use their own efficient written strategies to add integers and decimals.

Success criteria

The children have a **secure** level of attainment in relation to Objective 1 if the following question can be answered with a 'yes'.

Can the children...
... complete the assessment questions confidently and quickly by using an appropriate strategy for addition?

Administering the assessment

Discuss the layout of the Assessment sheet with the pupils, pointing out that space is provided for working out the answers. The assessment focuses on whether the pupils have an appropriate written strategy for addition of integers and decimals. Each child's strategy may be a method that the child has been shown in school or at home but this assessment is concerned with the requirement to use an 'efficient' written method. You may wish to refer to your school policy on calculation, which will specify an appropriate method. The final question is an extension activity as it puts the operation in the context of a problem. Some children will need help with reading the question.

(This assessment will also provide evidence for assessing strand 1, Using and applying mathematics: Solve multi-step problems, and problems involving fractions, decimals and percentages; choose and use appropriate calculation strategies at each stage.)

Answers: 31.415   52.369   25.46   5.559 kilometres

Andrew Brodie: Ten Minute Maths Assessments ages 10–11 © A&C Black 2009

Use efficient written methods to add integers and decimals

Name

Date

Look carefully at the addition questions.
Use the working out space to help you answer each question.

18.69 + 4.725 + 8

Answer

12 + 23.8 + 16.569

Answer

17 + 4.806 + 3.654

Answer

A boy walks 1.329 kilometres to school then 2.43 kilometres to football club. After football club he walks home, a distance of 1.8 kilometres. What is the total distance he walks?

Answer

I can use written methods for the addition of integers and decimals.

Use efficient written methods to subtract integers and decimals

Building on previous learning

Before starting this unit check that the children can already:

- derive and recall all addition and subtraction facts for each number to 20.
- derive and recall sums and differences of multiples of 10.
- derive and recall number pairs that total 100.
- identify the doubles of two-digit numbers and derive the corresponding halves.
- develop and use written methods to record, support or explain subtraction of two-digit and three-digit numbers.
- use mental methods for subtracting integers and decimals.

Learning objectives

Objective 1: Use efficient written methods to subtract integers and decimals.

Learning outcomes

The children will be able to:

- use their own efficient written strategies to subtract integers and decimals.

Success criteria

The children have a **secure** level of attainment in relation to Objective 1 if the following question can be answered with a 'yes'.

Can the children…

… complete the assessment questions confidently and quickly by using an appropriate strategy for subtraction?

Administering the assessment

Discuss the layout of the Assessment sheet with the pupils, pointing out that space is provided for working out the answers. The assessment focuses on whether the pupils have an appropriate written strategy for subtraction of integers and decimals. Each child's strategy may be a method they have been shown in school or at home but this assessment is concerned with the requirement to use an 'efficient' written method. You may wish to refer to your school policy on calculation, which will specify an appropriate method. The final question is an extension activity as it puts the operation in the context of a problem. Some children will need help with reading the question.

(This assessment will also provide evidence for assessing strand 1, Using and applying mathematics: Solve multi-step problems, and problems involving fractions, decimals and percentages; choose and use appropriate calculation strategies at each stage.)

Answers: *10.748*   *46.55*   *26.628*   *4575.76km*

Use efficient written methods to subtract integers and decimals

Name

Date

Look carefully at the subtraction questions.
Use the working out space to help you answer each question.

23.429 – 12.681

Answer

---

86 – 39.45

Answer

43.428 – 16.8

Answer

An aeroplane is flying from London to Muscat, a total distance of 5825.76 kilometres. When the plane has travelled 1250 kilometres how much further has it still to travel?

Answer

I can use written methods for the subtraction of integers and decimals.

Andrew Brodie: Ten Minute Maths Assessments ages 10–11 © A&C Black 2009

Use efficient written methods to multiply integers and decimals by a one-digit integer

Building on previous learning

Before starting this unit check that the children can already:
- recall multiplication facts up to 10 x 10.
- use written methods to record, support and explain multiplication of two-digit numbers by a one-digit number.
- use mental methods for multiplying numbers with decimals to one place by one-digit integers.

Learning objectives

Objective 1: Use efficient written methods to multiply integers and decimals by a one-digit integer.

Learning outcomes

The children will be able to:
- use their own efficient written strategies to multiply integers and decimals by a one-digit integer.

Success criteria

The children have a **secure** level of attainment in relation to Objective 1 if the following questions can be answered with a 'yes'.

Can the children...
... complete the assessment questions confidently and quickly by using an appropriate strategy for multiplication?

Administering the assessment

Discuss the layout of the Assessment sheet with the pupils, pointing out that space is provided for working out the answers. The assessment focuses on whether the pupils have an appropriate written strategy for multiplication of integers and decimals. Each child's strategy may be a method that they have been shown in school or at home but this assessment is concerned with the requirement to use an 'efficient written method'. You may wish to refer to your school policy on calculation, which will specify an appropriate method. The final question is an extension activity as it puts the operation in the context of a problem. Some children will need help with reading the question.

(This assessment will also provide evidence for assessing strand 1, Using and applying mathematics: Solve multi-step problems, and problems involving fractions, decimals and percentages; choose and use appropriate calculation strategies at each stage.)

Answers: 185.15   34.5   25.984   £58.05

Use efficient written methods to multiply integers and decimals by a one-digit integer

Name

Date

Look carefully at the multiplication questions.
Use the working out space to help you answer each question.

26.45 × 7

Answer

5.75 × 6

Answer

3.248 × 8

Answer

A poetry book costs £6.45
The headteacher decides to buy
9 copies of this book for the
school library. How much will they
cost altogether?

Answer

I can use written methods to multiply integers and decimals by a one-digit integer.

Use efficient written methods to divide integers and decimals by a one-digit integer

Building on previous learning

Before starting this unit check that the children can already:

- recall multiplication facts up to 10 x 10 and the corresponding division facts.
- use written methods to record, support and explain division of two-digit numbers by a one-digit number.
- use mental methods for dividing numbers with decimals to one place by one-digit integers.

Learning objectives

Objective 1: Use efficient written methods to divide integers and decimals by a one-digit integer.

Learning outcomes

The children will be able to:

- use their own efficient written strategies to divide integers and decimals by a one-digit integer.

Success criteria

The children have a **secure** level of attainment in relation to Objective 1 if the following question can be answered with a 'yes'.

Can the children…

… complete the assessment questions confidently and quickly by using an appropriate strategy for division?

Administering the assessment

Discuss the layout of the Assessment sheet with the pupils, pointing out that space is provided for working out the answers. The assessment focuses on whether the pupils have an appropriate written strategy for division of integers and decimals. Each child's strategy may be a method that they have been shown in school or at home but this assessment is concerned with the requirement to use an 'efficient written method'. You may wish to refer to your school policy on calculation, which will specify an appropriate method. The final question is an extension activity as it puts the operation in the context of a problem. Some children will need help with reading the question.

(This assessment will also provide evidence for assessing strand 1, Using and applying mathematics: Solve multi-step problems, and problems involving fractions, decimals and percentages; choose and use appropriate calculation strategies at each stage.)

Answers: *16.2* *9.5* *8.72* *£8.21*

Use efficient written methods to divide integers and decimals by a one-digit integer

Name

Date

Look carefully at the division questions.
Use the working out space to help you answer each question.

48.6 ÷ 3

Answer

85.5 ÷ 9

Answer

61.04 ÷ 7

Answer

Grandmother has £32.84 in her money box. She shares the money equally between her four grandchildren. How much money does each grandchild receive?

Answer

I can use written methods to divide integers and decimals by a one-digit integer.

Use efficient written methods to multiply two-digit and three-digit integers by a two-digit integer

Building on previous learning

Before starting this unit check that the children can already:
- recall multiplication facts up to 10 x 10.
- use written methods to record, support and explain multiplication of two-digit numbers by a one-digit number.

Learning objectives

Objective 1: Use efficient written methods to multiply two-digit and three-digit integers by a two-digit integer.

Learning outcomes

The children will be able to:
- use their own efficient written strategies to multiply two-digit and three-digit integers by a two-digit integer.

Success criteria

The children have a **secure** level of attainment in relation to Objective 1 if the following question can be answered with a 'yes'.

Can the children...
... complete the assessment questions confidently and quickly by using an appropriate strategy for multiplication?

Administering the assessment

Discuss the layout of the Assessment sheet with the pupils, pointing out that space is provided for working out the answers. The assessment focuses on whether the pupils have an appropriate written strategy for multiplication of two-digit and three-digit integers by a two-digit integer. Each child's strategy may be a method that they have been shown in school or at home but this assessment is concerned with the requirement to use an 'efficient written method'. You may wish to refer to your school policy on calculation, which will specify an appropriate method. The final question is an extension activity as it puts the operation in the context of a problem. Some children will need help with reading the question.

(This assessment will also provide evidence for assessing strand 1, Using and applying mathematics: Solve multi-step problems, and problems involving fractions, decimals and percentages; choose and use appropriate calculation strategies at each stage.)

Answers: 1682   13505   30996   £2388

Use efficient written methods to multiply two-digit and three-digit integers by a two-digit integer

Name

Date

Look carefully at the multiplication questions.
Use the working out space to help you answer each question.

58 x 29

Answer

365 x 37

Answer

492 x 63

Answer

A new computer costs £398. The headteacher decides to buy 6 of these computers for Class 1. How much will they cost altogether?

Answer

I can use written methods to multiply multiply two-digit and three-digit integers by a two-digit integer.

Express a quotient as a fraction or a decimal

Building on previous learning

Before starting this unit check that the children can already:

- recall multiplication facts up to 10 x 10 and the corresponding division facts.
- use written methods to record, support and explain division of two-digit numbers by a one-digit number.
- use mental methods for dividing numbers with decimals to one place by one-digit integers.
- use efficient written methods to divide integers and decimals by a one-digit integer.

Learning objectives

Objective 1: Express a quotient as a fraction or a decimal.

Learning outcomes

The children will be able to:

- record the result of a division in one of three ways: with a remainder, as a decimal or as a fraction.

Success criteria

The children have a **secure** level of attainment in relation to Objective 1 if the following questions can be answered with a 'yes'.

Can the children…

… complete the assessment questions to produce answers with remainders?

… complete the assessment questions to produce answers as decimals?

… complete the assessment questions to produce answers as fractions?

Administering the assessment

Discuss the layout of the Assessment sheet with the pupils, pointing out that space is provided for working out the answers to the questions. You may decide to allow the pupils to use a calculator for the questions. The assessment focuses on how pupils deal with the result of their calculations. Encourage the pupils to explain when it may be appropriate to give a remainder e.g. when sharing out whole items that cannot be broken or split, when it may be appropriate to give a decimal answer e.g. when sharing money, or when it may be appropriate to give a fractional answer e.g. when sharing bars of chocolate.

(This assessment will also provide evidence for assessing strand 1, Using and applying mathematics: Solve multi-step problems, and problems involving fractions, decimals and percentages; choose and use appropriate calculation strategies at each stage, including calculator use.)

Answers: 5 remainder 3 or 5.5 or $5\frac{1}{2}$

11 remainder 3 or 11.6 or $11\frac{3}{5}$

33 remainder 1 or 33.5 or $33\frac{1}{2}$

18 remainder 1 or 18.25 or $18\frac{1}{4}$

5 remainder 5 or 5.625 or $5\frac{5}{8}$

Andrew Brodie: Ten Minute Maths Assessments ages 10–11 © A&C Black 2009

Express a quotient as a fraction or a decimal

Name

Date

Look at this division question.

23 ÷ 4

The answer to this can be given as   **5 remainder 3**   or   **5.75**   or   **5$\frac{3}{4}$**

For each question below, give the answer in three ways.

33 ÷ 6

---   --------------   --------------

58 ÷ 5

---   --------------   --------------

67 ÷ 2

---   --------------   --------------

73 ÷ 4

---   --------------   --------------

45 ÷ 8

---   --------------   --------------

I can use division to produce answers that include fractions or decimals.

Find fractions of whole number quantities

Building on previous learning

Before starting this unit check that the children can already:
- derive and recall multiplication facts up to 10 x 10, and the corresponding division facts.
- read and write proper fractions.
- find fractions of numbers, quantities or shapes.

Learning objectives

Objective 1: Find fractions of whole number quantities.
Objective 2: Use a calculator to solve problems involving multi-step calculations.

Learning outcomes

The children will be able to:
- find fractions of whole number quantities e.g. $\frac{5}{8}$ of 96.

Success criteria

The children have a **secure** level of attainment in relation to the Objective 1 if the following question can be answered with a 'yes'.

Can the children…
… complete the assessment question confidently and quickly, using the calculator where appropriate?

Administering the assessment

Ensure that the children understand how to show their answers on the Assessment sheet. Discuss the following question, explaining that the answer could be given with two different units: How much is two fifths of 1 kilogram? (The answer could be given as 0.4kg or 400g.) Both of these answers are correct and either is acceptable. Encourage the pupils to be aware of the appropriate units when answering questions relating to quantities. They may use calculators for this assessment but encourage them to make their own decision when best to use mental arithmetic and when best to use calculators.

Question 1: What is one quarter of 32?	8
Question 2: What is one quarter of 240?	60
Question 3: What is three quarters of 240?	180
Question 4: What is one eighth of 96?	12
Question 5: What is five eighths of 96?	60
Question 6: What is five sixths of 30?	25
Question 7: What is three eighths of 72?	27
Question 8: What is four sevenths of 35?	20
Question 9: What is five ninths of 27?	15
Question 10: How much is three quarters of £32?	£24
Question 11: How much is two thirds of £42?	£28
Question 12: How much is four fifths of £60?	£48
Question 13: How much is three tenths of £65?	£19.50
Question 14: How far is four fifths of 2000 kilometres?	1600km
Question 15: How much is three quarters of 1.2 kilograms?	900g

(This assessment will also provide evidence for assessing strand 1, Using and applying mathematics: Solve multi-step problems, and problems involving fractions, decimals and percentages; choose and use appropriate calculation strategies at each stage, including calculator use.)

Andrew Brodie: Ten Minute Maths Assessments ages 10–11 © A&C Black 2009

Find fractions of whole number quantities

Name

Date

Write the answers to the questions in the correct boxes.

1. What is one quarter of 32?

2. What is one quarter of 240?

3. What is three quarters of 240?

4. What is one eighth of 96?

5. What is five eighths of 96?

6. What is five sixths of 30?

7. What is three eighths of 72?

8. What is four sevenths of 35?

9. What is five ninths of 27?

10. How much is three quarters of £32?

11. How much is two thirds of £42?

12. How much is four fifths of £60?

13. How much is three tenths of £65?

14. How far is four fifths of 2000 km?

15. How much is three quarters of 1.2 kg?

I can find fractions of whole number quantities.

Find percentages of whole number quantities

Building on previous learning

Before starting this unit check that the children can already:

- derive and recall multiplication facts up to 10 x 10, and the corresponding division facts.
- use understanding of place value to divide whole numbers and decimals by 10.
- use mental methods for multiplying whole numbers.
- find common percentages (10%, 50%, 25%, 5%, 15%) of numbers and quantities.

Learning objectives

Objective 1: Find percentages of whole number quantities.

Learning outcomes

The children will be able to:

- find percentages of whole number quantities e.g. 35% of £70.

Success criteria

The children have a **secure** level of attainment in relation to Objective 1 if the following question can be answered with a 'yes'.

Can the children...

... complete the assessment questions confidently and quickly, without using a calculator?

Administering the assessment

Ensure that the children understand how to show their answers on the Assessment sheet. They should *not* use a calculator for this assessment. The purpose of the assessment is to establish whether the pupils understand percentage, and how to find percentages of quantities by relating specified percentages to 10%, 25% or 50% e.g. to find 65% of a quantity the pupils could find 10% of the quantity and multiply it by 6.5. You may decide to discuss the first three questions with the pupils, encouraging them to notice how the first question gives a clue to the second and how the first two can help with the third.

Question 1: What is 10% of £30?	*£3*
Question 2: What is 5% of £30?	*£1.50*
Question 3: What is 15% of £30?	*£4.50*
Question 4: What is 10% of £70?	*£7*
Question 5: What is 30% of £70?	*£21*
Question 6: What is 5% of £70?	*£3.50*
Question 7: What is 35% of £70?	*£24.50*
Question 8: What is 10% of £260?	*£26*
Question 9: What is 5% of £260?	*£13*
Question 10: What is 60% of £260?	*£156*
Question 11: What is 65% of £260?	*£169*
Question 12: What is 40% of £300?	*£120*
Question 13: What is 70% of £800?	*£560*
Question 14: What is 90% of £500?	*£450*
Question 15: What is 15% of £600?	*£90*

(This assessment will also provide evidence for assessing strand 1, Using and applying mathematics: Solve multi-step problems, and problems involving fractions, decimals and percentages; choose and use appropriate calculation strategies at each stage.)

Andrew Brodie: Ten Minute Maths Assessments ages 10–11 © A&C Black 2009

Find percentages of whole number quantities

Name

Date

Write the answers to the questions in the correct boxes.

1. What is 10% of £30?

2. What is 5% of £30?

3. What is 15% of £30?

4. What is 10% of £70?

5. What is 30% of £70?

6. What is 5% of £70?

7. What is 35% of £70?

8. What is 10% of £260?

9. What is 5% of £260?

10. What is 60% of £260?

11. What is 65% of £260?

12. What is 40% of £300?

13. What is 70% of £800?

14. What is 90% of £500?

15. What is 15% of £600?

I can find percentages of whole number quantities.

Andrew Brodie: Ten Minute Maths Assessments ages 10–11 © A&C Black 2009

Use a calculator to solve problems

Building on previous learning

Before starting this unit check that the children can already:
- use knowledge of rounding, number operations and inverses to estimate and check calculations.
- find percentages of whole number quantities.

Learning objectives

Objective 1: Use a calculator to solve problems involving multi-step calculations.

Learning outcomes

The children will be able to:
- use a calculator to solve problems involving multi-step calculations, including those involving percentages or fractions.

Success criteria

The children have a **secure** level of attainment in relation to Objective 1 if the following questions can be answered with a 'yes'.

Can the children...
... complete the assessment questions using a systematic step-by-step approach?
... use the calculator appropriately to find fractions or percentages of quantities or amounts?
... solve multi-step problems?

Administering the assessment

Some children will need help with reading the questions. Read each question through with them several times so that they understand the problem and the context in which it is set. What is needed is a step-by-step approach involving appropriate calculations and jottings e.g. in the first question, do the children realise that they need to work out $\frac{5}{6}$ of 30 and 70% of 30 in order to make comparisons?

(This assessment will also provide evidence for assessing strand 1, Using and applying mathematics: Solve multi-step problems, and problems involving fractions, decimals and percentages; choose and use appropriate calculation strategies at each stage, including calculator use; Tabulate systematically the information in a problem or puzzle; identify and record the steps or calculations needed to solve it, using symbols where appropriate; interpret solutions in the original context and check their accuracy; Explain reasoning and conclusions, using words, symbols or diagrams as appropriate.)

Answers:　Asif had a score of 18/30, Ben had a score of 25/30 and Carl had a score of 21/30 so Ben had the highest score and Asif had the lowest. The order was Ben, Carl, Asif.

The total full price cost of the two items was £343. The saving will be 20% of £343 = £68.60. The total price to pay will be £343 - £68.60 = £274.40

Use a calculator to solve problems

Name

Date

Asif, Ben and Carl had a test. There were 30 questions in the test.
Asif got 18 questions correct. Ben got five sixths of the questions correct.
Carl got 70% of the questions correct.

Out of the three children who got the highest score in the test?

Who got the lowest score?

Write the three children in the order of their scores, highest first.

----------------------------   ------------------------------   ------------------------------

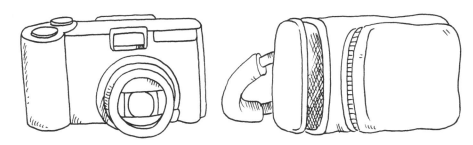

A camera costs £298. The camera bag to go with it costs £45. The shop
manager says he will give you a discount of 20% off your total bill if you buy
both items together. How much will you pay if you buy both items together?

I can use a calculator to solve problems.

Andrew Brodie: Ten Minute Maths Assessments ages 10–11 © A&C Black 2009

Visualise and draw on grids of different types where a shape will be after reflection

Building on previous learning

Before starting this unit check that the children can already:
- describe, visualise, classify and draw 2-D shapes.
- sort, make and describe shapes, referring to their properties.
- identify reflective symmetry in patterns.
- identify reflective symmetry in 2-D shapes and draw lines of symmetry in shapes.
- draw the position of a shape after a reflection.

Learning objectives

Objective 1: Visualise and draw on grids of different types where a shape will be after reflection.

Learning outcomes

The children will be able to:
- identify the x-axis and y-axis.
- draw the reflection of the shape in the x-axis and y-axis.

Success criteria

The children have a **secure** level of attainment in relation to Objective 1 if the following questions can be answered with a 'yes'.

Can the children…
… understand the vocabulary of reflection *in* a specified line?
… draw the reflection of the triangle in each axis?

Administering the assessment

Discuss the Assessment sheet with the pupils ensuring that they understand the vocabulary: *x*-axis, *y*-axis, reflection in. As an extension activity you could ask the children to draw the reflection of the triangle in the line *x* = 2 or in the line *y* = 4. You may also wish to supply the children with some triangular grid paper (see page 96) and ask them to draw reflections in specified lines.

(This assessment will also provide evidence for assessing strand 1, Using and applying mathematics: Represent and interpret sequences, patterns and relationships involving numbers and shapes.)

Answers:

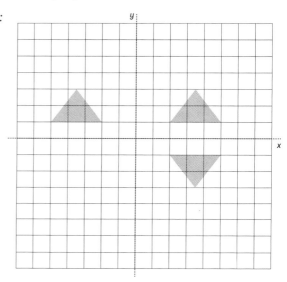

Visualise and draw on grids of different types where a shape will be after reflection

Name

Date

Look at the grid. Find the *x*-axis and the *y*-axis.
Draw the reflection of the triangle in the *x*-axis.

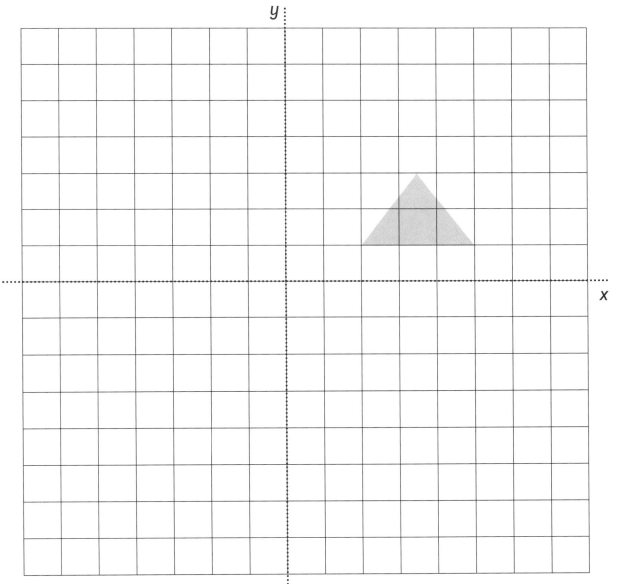

Now draw the reflection of the triangle in the *y*-axis.

I can draw the position of a shape after a reflection.

Visualise and draw on grids of different types where a shape will be after translations

Building on previous learning

Before starting this unit check that the children can already:

- describe, visualise, classify and draw 2-D shapes.
- sort, make and describe shapes, referring to their properties.
- identify reflective symmetry in patterns.
- identify reflective symmetry in 2-D shapes and draw lines of symmetry in shapes.
- draw the position of a shape after a reflection.

Learning objectives

Objective 1: Visualise and draw on grids of different types where a shape will be after translations.

Learning outcomes

The children will be able to:

- describe the effects of translations.
- draw the position of a shape after translations.

Success criteria

The children have a **secure** level of attainment in relation to Objective 1 if the following questions can be answered with a 'yes'.

Can the children...

... understand the vocabulary of translations?

... describe the translation needed to move triangle A to the position of triangle B?

... draw the position of triangle C after two translations?

Administering the assessment

Discuss the Assessment sheet with the pupils ensuring that they understand the vocabulary: x-axis, y-axis, translation. As an extension activity you could ask the children to draw further positions of the shapes after specified translations.

(This assessment will also provide evidence for assessing strand 1, Using and applying mathematics: Represent and interpret sequences, patterns and relationships involving numbers and shapes.)

Answers: Triangle A has been translated 5 squares to the right and 11 squares up.

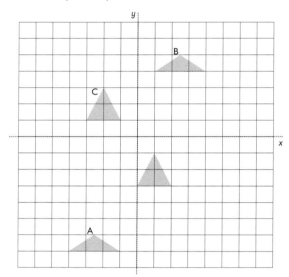

Visualise and draw where a shape will be after translations

Name

Date

Describe the translations that would move triangle A to the exact position of triangle B.

....

....

Now translate triangle C three squares to the right and four squares down.

I can describe translations.

I can draw the position of a shape after translations.

Visualise and draw on grids of different types where a shape will be after rotation through 90° or 180°

Building on previous learning

Before starting this unit check that the children can already:
- describe, visualise, classify and draw 2-D shapes.
- sort, make and describe shapes, referring to their properties.
- identify reflective symmetry in patterns.
- identify reflective symmetry in 2-D shapes and draw lines of symmetry in shapes.
- draw the position of a shape after a reflection.
- draw the position of a shape after translations.

Learning objectives

Objective 1: Visualise and draw on grids of different types where a shape will be after rotation through 90° or 180° about its centre or one of its vertices.

Learning outcomes

The children will be able to:
- draw the position of a shape after a rotation of 90° or 180° about a specified vertex.
- draw the position of a shape after a rotation of 90° about its centre.

Success criteria

The children have a **secure** level of attainment in relation to Objective 1 if the following questions can be answered with a 'yes'.

Can the children...
... understand the vocabulary of rotation?
... draw the positions of the rectangles after the specified rotations?

Administering the assessment

Discuss the Assessment sheet with the pupils ensuring that they understand the vocabulary: x-axis, y-axis, rotation, vertex, centre. As an extension activity you could ask the children to draw further positions of the shapes after specified rotations.

(This assessment will also provide evidence for assessing strand 1, Using and applying mathematics: Represent and interpret sequences, patterns and relationships involving numbers and shapes.)

Answers:

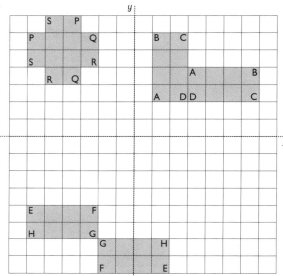

Visualise and draw where a shape will be after rotation through 90° or 180°

Name

Date

Draw the rotation of the rectangle ABCD 90° anticlockwise about the vertex D.

Draw the rotation of the rectangle EFGH 180° clockwise about the vertex G.

Draw the rotation of the rectangle PQRS 90° clockwise about its centre.

I can draw the position of a shape after rotation.

Use coordinates in the first quadrant to draw, locate and complete shapes that meet given properties

Building on previous learning

Before starting this unit check that the children can already:

- describe, visualise, classify and draw 2-D shapes.
- sort, make and describe shapes, referring to their properties.
- read and plot coordinates in the first quadrant.

Learning objectives

Objective 1: Use coordinates in the first quadrant to draw, locate and complete shapes that meet given properties.

Learning outcomes

The children will be able to:

- state the coordinates of given points.
- select appropriate coordinates to complete the drawing of a shape.
- use their knowledge of symmetry.

Success criteria

The children have a **secure** level of attainment in relation to Objective 1 if the following questions can be answered with a 'yes'.

Can the children…

… identify the position of any point on the grid by using coordinates, giving the x value before the y value?

… write the coordinates correctly, within brackets and separated by commas?

… use their knowledge and understanding of symmetry to complete the hexagon on the grid?

Administering the assessment

Discuss the Assessment sheet with the pupils ensuring that they understand the vocabulary: x-axis, y-axis, coordinates, the line x = 7 and the line y = 7.

(This assessment will also provide evidence for assessing strand 1, Using and applying mathematics: Represent and interpret sequences, patterns and relationships involving numbers and shapes.)

Answers:

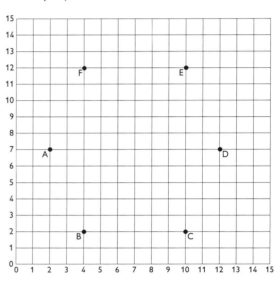

Use coordinates in the first quadrant to draw, locate and complete shapes that meet given properties

Name _____

Date _____

Look at the grid.

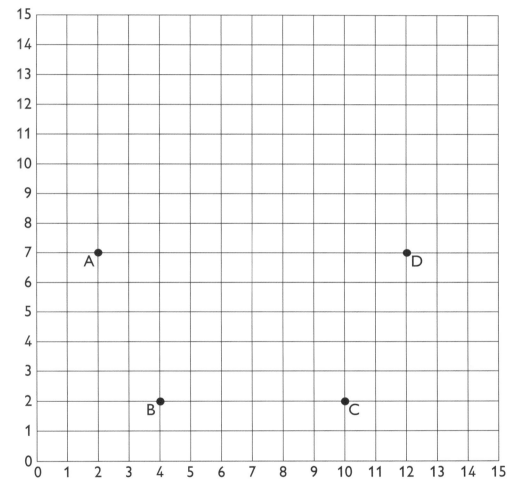

Give the coordinates of the four points:

A _____ **B** _____ **C** _____ **D** _____

Draw and label the points E and F so that the points A, B, C, D, E and F can be joined together to create a hexagon. The hexagon should be symmetrical about the line $x = 7$ and the line $y = 7$.

I can identify coordinates in the first quadrant.

I can use coordinates to draw shapes that meet given properties.

Estimate angles, and use a protractor to measure and draw them, on their own and in shapes

Building on previous learning

Before starting this unit check that the children can already:

- use a set-square to draw right angles.
- identify right angles in 2-D shapes.
- compare angles with a right angle.
- calculate angles in a straight line.
- compare and order angles less than 180°.
- know that angles are measured in degrees and that one whole turn is 360°.

Learning objectives

Objective 1: Estimate angles, and use a protractor to measure and draw them, on their own and in shapes.

Learning outcomes

The children will be able to:

- estimate and measure angles using a protractor to a suitable degree of accuracy.
- draw lines at specified angles.
- measure angles in a shape.

Success criteria

The children have a **secure** level of attainment in relation to Objective 1 if the following questions can be answered with a 'yes'.

Can the children…
… state whether each angle is acute or obtuse?
… make effective estimates of the angles shown?
… measure the angles accurately?
… measure the angles in the quadrilateral?

Administering the assessment

Ensure that the children understand that they must make an estimate and then measure each angle. Watch carefully how they use the protractor. Many children make mistakes because they don't understand the calibration on the protractor. The pupils' measurements of the four angles of the quadrilateral will probably not add up to 360° as the angles are very difficult to measure totally accurately. To complete the assessment, ask the pupils to draw pairs of lines at the following angles:

38°   125°   91°   210°

(This assessment will also provide evidence for assessing strand 1, Using and applying mathematics: Represent and interpret sequences, patterns and relationships involving numbers and shapes.)

Answers: 45°   60°   76°   135°   167°
            125°   96°   108°   31°

Estimate angles, and use a protractor to measure them

Name

Date

Look at the angles. Write an estimate for the size of each angle and then measure the angle carefully.

estimated size: _____

actual size: _____

estimated size: _____

actual size: _____

estimated size: _____

actual size: _____

estimated size: _____

actual size: _____

estimated size: _____

actual size: _____

Look at the shape.
Measure each angle.

Add these four angles together. What is the total?

I can estimate the size of angles.

I can measure angles accurately.

I can measure angles in shapes.

Andrew Brodie: Ten Minute Maths Assessments ages 10–11 © A&C Black 2009

Calculate angles in a triangle or around a point

Building on previous learning

Before starting this unit check that the children can already:
- calculate angles in a straight line.
- compare and order angles less than 180°.
- compare angles with a right angle.
- estimate angles, and use a protractor to measure and draw them, on their own and in shapes.
- use a calculator to solve problems involving multi-step calculations.
- use approximations and inverse operations to estimate and check results.

Learning objectives

Objective 1: Calculate angles in a triangle or around a point.

Learning outcomes

The children will be able to:
- calculate angles in a triangle.
- calculate angles around a point.
- use approximations and inverse operations to estimate and check results.

Success criteria

The children have a **secure** level of attainment in relation to Objective 1 if the following questions can be answered with a 'yes'.

Can the children...
- ... make sensible estimates for the missing angle in each triangle on the Assessment sheet?
- ... calculate each angle accurately?
- ... make sensible estimates for the missing angle around each point on the Assessment sheet?
- ... calculate each angle accurately?

Administering the assessment

Ensure that the children are aware that the three angles of every triangle add up to 180° and that the angles around a point add up to 360°. The assessment encourages children to estimate the size of each missing angle first as this will help them to decide whether the result of their calculation is correct.

(This assessment will also provide evidence for assessing strand 1, Using and applying mathematics: Solve multi-step problems, and problems involving fractions, decimals and percentages; choose and use appropriate calculation strategies at each stage, including calculator use; Tabulate systematically the information in a problem or puzzle; identify and record the steps or calculations needed to solve it, using symbols where appropriate; interpret solutions in the original context and check their accuracy; Suggest, plan and develop lines of enquiry; collect, organise and represent information, interpret results and review methods; identify and answer related questions; Represent and interpret sequences, patterns and relationships involving numbers and shapes; suggest and test hypotheses; construct and use simple expressions and formulae in words then symbols; Explain reasoning and conclusions, using words, symbols or diagrams as appropriate.)

Answers: 75°   66°
               45°   99°

Andrew Brodie: Ten Minute Maths Assessments ages 10–11 © A&C Black 2009

Calculate angles in a triangle or around a point

Name

Date

Look at each triangle. Estimate the size of the missing angle before calculating it.

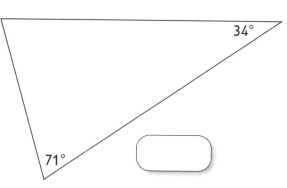

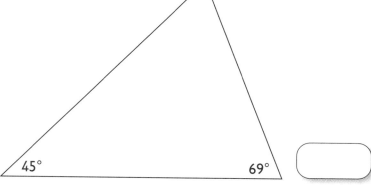

Look at the angles around each point.
Estimate the size of the missing angle before calculating it.

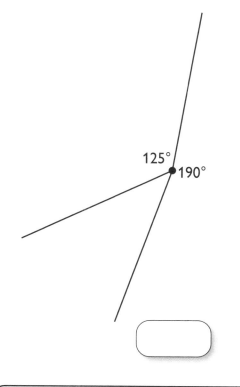

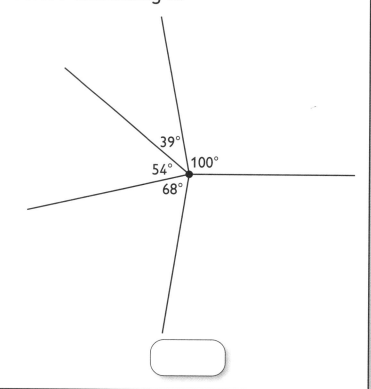

I can calculate angles in a triangle.

I can calculate angles around a point.

Andrew Brodie: Ten Minute Maths Assessments ages 10–11 © A&C Black 2009

Convert between units using decimals to two places

Building on previous learning

Before starting this unit check that the children can already:
- calculate mentally with integers and decimals.
- use understanding of place value to multiply and divide whole numbers and decimals by 10, 100 or 1000.

Learning objectives

Objective 1: Convert between units using decimals to two places.

Learning outcomes

The children will be able to:
- use mental methods and understanding of place value to multiply and divide whole numbers and decimals by 10, 100 or 1000 to convert between units using decimals to two places.

Success criteria

The children have a **secure** level of attainment in relation to Objective 1 if the following question can be answered with a 'yes'.

Can the children...
... respond quickly and accurately to the questions on the CD?

Administering the assessment

Track 15 Ensure that the children understand the task. A period of ten seconds is allowed for each question but you may need to pause the CD for some questions. This is the script for the CD if you decide to dictate the questions (the answers are provided after each question below).

Question 1: Convert 3.5 metres to centimetres	350cm
Question 2: Convert 2.5 metres to millimetres	2500mm
Question 3: Convert 3.79 metres to centimetres	379cm
Question 4: Convert 4.65 metres to millimetres	4650mm
Question 5: Convert 3250 millimetres to metres	3.25m
Question 6: Convert 516 centimetres to metres	5.16m
Question 7: Convert 4.7 centimetres to millimetres	47mm
Question 8: Convert 18 centimetres to metres	0.18m
Question 9: Convert 3 centimetres to metres	0.03m
Question 10: Convert 4.6 kilograms to grams	4600g
Question 11: Convert 7.25 kilograms to grams	7250g
Question 12: Convert 0.65 kilograms to grams	650g
Question 13: Convert 2060 grams to kilograms	2.06kg
Question 14: Convert 850 grams to kilograms	0.85kg
Question 15: Convert 3.75 litres to millilitres	3750ml
Question 16: Convert 2.9 litres to millilitres	2900ml
Question 17: Convert 0.5 litres to millilitres	500ml
Question 18: Convert 0.89 litres to millilitres	890ml
Question 19: Convert 250 millilitres to litres	0.25l
Question 20: Convert 20 millilitres to litres	0.02l

(This assessment will also provide evidence for assessing strand 1, Using and applying mathematics: Solve multi-step problems, and problems involving fractions, decimals and percentages; choose and use appropriate calculation strategies at each stage.)

Andrew Brodie: Ten Minute Maths Assessments ages 10–11 © A&C Black 2009

Convert between units using decimals to two places

Name

Date

Listen carefully to the CD or your teacher.
Write the answers to the questions in the correct boxes.

1. [ ] 3.5 m

2. [ ] 2.5 m

3. [ ] 3.79 m

4. [ ] 4.65 m

5. [ ] 3250 mm

6. [ ] 516 cm

7. [ ] 4.7 cm

8. [ ] 18 cm

9. [ ] 3 cm

10. [ ] 4. 6kg

11. [ ] 7.25 kg

12. [ ] 0.65 kg

13. [ ] 2060 g

14. [ ] 850 g

15. [ ] 3.75 l

16. [ ] 2.9 l

17. [ ] 0.5 l

18. [ ] 0.89 l

19. [ ] 250 ml

20. [ ] 20 ml

I can convert between units using decimals to two places. [ ]

Calculate the perimeter and area of rectilinear shapes

Building on previous learning

Before starting this unit check that the children can already:

- calculate mentally with integers and decimals.
- use efficient written methods to add integers and decimals.
- use a calculator to solve problems involving multi-step calculations.

Learning objectives

Objective 1: Calculate the perimeter and area of rectilinear shapes.

Learning outcomes

The children will be able to:

- measure the sides of the rectangles accurately and use these measurements to calculate the perimeters by adding or the areas by multiplying.

Success criteria

The children have a **secure** level of attainment in relation to Objective 1 if the following questions can be answered with a 'yes'.

Can the children…

… measure the sides of the rectangles accurately?

… add the lengths of the four sides together to find the perimeter of each rectangle?

… multiply the length of the base by the length of the height to find the area of each rectangle?

Administering the assessment

Ensure that the children understand the task. Many children get perimeter and area confused and you could discuss the idea of a 'perimeter fence' to help them understand that the perimeter is a measurement of length. The perimeter should be shown in centimetres and the area should be shown in square centimetres.

(This assessment will also provide evidence for assessing strand 1, Using and applying mathematics: Solve multi-step problems, and problems involving fractions, decimals and percentages; choose and use appropriate calculation strategies at each stage, including calculator use; Tabulate systematically the information in a problem or puzzle; identify and record the steps or calculations needed to solve it, using symbols where appropriate; interpret solutions in the original context and check their accuracy; Suggest, plan and develop lines of enquiry; collect, organise and represent information, interpret results and review methods; identify and answer related questions; Represent and interpret sequences, patterns and relationships involving numbers and shapes; suggest and test hypotheses; construct and use simple expressions and formulae in words then symbols; Explain reasoning and conclusions, using words, symbols or diagrams as appropriate.)

Answers: Perimeter = 31.4cm   Area = 55.12cm^2
          Perimeter = 30cm   Area = 37.76cm^2

Calculate the perimeter and area of rectilinear shapes

Name

Date

Measure the lengths of the sides of each of the rectangles.

What is the perimeter of each rectangle?

What is the area of each rectangle?

perimeter = [   ]   area = [   ]

perimeter = [   ]   area = [   ]

I can calculate the perimeter of rectilinear shapes.

I can calculate the area of rectilinear shapes.

Estimate the area of an irregular shape by counting squares

Building on previous learning

Before starting this unit check that the children can already:
- calculate the perimeter and area of rectilinear shapes.

Learning objectives

Objective 1: Estimate the area of an irregular shape by counting squares.

Learning outcomes

The children will be able to:
- count whole squares and round all part squares to half-squares.

Success criteria

The children have a **secure** level of attainment in relation to Objective 1 if the following questions can be answered with a 'yes'.

Can the children...
... count the whole squares accurately?
... consider each part square as a half-square and count these accurately?
... combine the whole squares and half-squares to find a realistic estimate of the area of the leaf?

Administering the assessment

Ensure that the children understand the task and that they are familiar with the idea of considering part squares as half-squares.

(This assessment will also provide evidence for assessing strand 1, Using and applying mathematics: Solve multi-step problems, and problems involving fractions, decimals and percentages; choose and use appropriate calculation strategies at each stage, including calculator use; Tabulate systematically the information in a problem or puzzle; identify and record the steps or calculations needed to solve it, using symbols where appropriate; interpret solutions in the original context and check their accuracy; Suggest, plan and develop lines of enquiry; collect, organise and represent information, interpret results and review methods; identify and answer related questions; Represent and interpret sequences, patterns and relationships involving numbers and shapes; suggest and test hypotheses; construct and use simple expressions and formulae in words then symbols; Explain reasoning and conclusions, using words, symbols or diagrams as appropriate.)

Answer: *Estimated area = 84 square centimetres*

Estimate the area of an irregular shape by counting squares

Name

Date

Estimate the area of the leaf.

Estimated
area = _____

I can estimate the area of an irregular shape by counting squares.

Andrew Brodie: Ten Minute Maths Assessments ages 10–11 © A&C Black 2009

Describe and predict outcomes from data using the language of chance or likelihood

Building on previous learning

Before starting this unit check that the children can already:
- describe the occurrence of familiar events using the language of chance or likelihood.

Learning objectives

Objective 1: Describe and predict outcomes from data using the language of chance or likelihood.

Learning outcomes

The children will be able to:
- use appropriate vocabulary when describing probabilities.
- make appropriate predictions of probability.
- experiment and record results effectively.

Success criteria

The children have a **secure** level of attainment in relation to Objective 1 if the following questions can be answered with a 'yes'.

Can the children…
- … use appropriate vocabulary, such as likely, unlikely, equally likely, certain, impossible, chance, even chance, fifty-fifty chance, etc, when describing probabilities?
- … make appropriate predictions of probability, for example the probability of rolling a 2?
- … experiment and record results effectively?

Administering the assessment

Ensure that the children understand the task. Use the opportunity to discuss the assessments with them to check that they are using appropriate vocabulary.

(This assessment will also provide evidence for assessing strand 1, Using and applying mathematics: Solve multi-step problems, and problems involving fractions; choose and use appropriate calculation strategies at each stage; Tabulate systematically the information in a problem or puzzle; identify and record the steps or calculations needed to solve it, using symbols where appropriate; interpret solutions in the original context and check their accuracy; Suggest, plan and develop lines of enquiry; collect, organise and represent information, interpret results and review methods; identify and answer related questions; Represent and interpret sequences, patterns and relationships involving numbers and shapes; suggest and test hypotheses; construct and use simple expressions and formulae in words then symbols; Explain reasoning and conclusions, using words, symbols or diagrams as appropriate.)

Answers: *certain or 6/6*
　　　　　impossible or 0/6
　　　　　1/6
　　　　　1/6
　　　　　3/6 or 1/2
　　　　　1/6
　　　　　Prediction should be 5 times. Final answer will depend on experiment.

Andrew Brodie: Ten Minute Maths Assessments ages 10–11 © A&C Black 2009

Describe and predict outcomes from data using the language of chance or likelihood

Name

Date

Look at the dice.
It is an ordinary dice with six faces.

If I roll this dice once…

What is the probability of rolling a number that is less than 7?

What is the probability of rolling a number that is more than 20?

What is the probability of rolling a 5?

What is the probability of rolling a 2?

What is the probability of rolling a multiple of 2?

What is the probability of rolling a 6?

You are going to roll the dice 30 times.
Predict how many times you will roll a 6.

Now, roll the dice 30 times and record your outcomes.
How many times did you roll a 6?

I can describe and predict outcomes from data using the language of chance or likelihood.

Describe and interpret results and solutions to problems using the mode, range, median and mean

Building on previous learning

Before starting this unit check that the children can already:
- find and interpret the mode of a set of data.

Learning objectives

Objective 1: Describe and interpret results and solutions to problems using the mode, range, median and mean.

Learning outcomes

The children will be able to:
- use appropriate vocabulary when handling data.
- find the mode, range, median and mean of a set of data.

Success criteria

The children have a **secure** level of attainment in relation to Objective 1 if the following questions can be answered with a 'yes'.

Can the children...

... use appropriate vocabulary, such as mode, range, median, mean and average?

... interpret the data, finding the mode, range, median and mean by using appropriate calculations where necessary?

... organise the data to make it easier to interpret, e.g. by arranging in rank order?

Administering the assessment

Ensure that the children understand the task. Use the opportunity to discuss the assessments with them to check that they are using appropriate vocabulary.

(This assessment will also provide evidence for assessing strand 1, Using and applying mathematics: Solve multi-step problems, and problems involving fractions; choose and use appropriate calculation strategies at each stage; Tabulate systematically the information in a problem or puzzle; identify and record the steps or calculations needed to solve it, using symbols where appropriate; interpret solutions in the original context and check their accuracy; Suggest, plan and develop lines of enquiry; collect, organise and represent information, interpret results and review methods; identify and answer related questions; Represent and interpret sequences, patterns and relationships involving numbers and shapes; suggest and test hypotheses; construct and use simple expressions and formulae in words then symbols; Explain reasoning and conclusions, using words, symbols or diagrams as appropriate.)

Answers: Georgia
Humphrey
Range: 20 − 8 = 12
Yes, mode = 18
Median = 13
Den
Mean = 14

Describe and interpret results and solutions to problems using the mode, range, median and mean

Name

Date

9 children had a spelling test. The maximum score was 20.
Here are their results:

Ahmed	16
Ben	11
Claire	18
Den	13
Ella	10
Farhan	18
Georgia	20
Humphrey	8
Imogen	12

Who had the highest score? _____

Who had the lowest score? _____

What was the range of
the scores? _____

Is there a mode? _____

If 'yes', what is it? _____

What is the median score? _____

Who has the median score? _____

What is the mean score? _____

I can find the mode of a set of data, if there is a mode.

I can find the range of a set of data.

I can find the median of a set of data.

I can find the mean of a set of data.

Triangular grid paper

Andrew Brodie: Ten Minute Maths Assessments ages 10–11 © A&C Black 2009